Good News
For the World

Gerard Fourez

Sheed & Ward

Sheed and Ward™ is a service of National Catholic Reporter Publishing, Inc.

Library of Congress Catalog Card Number: 85-62338

ISBN: 0-934134-52-9

Published by: Sheed and Ward
            115 E. Armour Blvd., P.O. Box 281
            Kansas City, MO 64141-0281

To order, call: 800-821-7926

Contents

iii

PART III: Existential Concepts and Theology

First the spirit became a camel.
Then the camel became a lion.
Then the lion became a child.

> Nietzsche in *"So Sprach Zarathustra."*
> (The three metamorphoses of the Spirit)

If you do not become like a child, you
will not enter the Kingdom of Heaven. *(Matthew, 18:3.)*

PREFACE

It is not easy to recognize the Gospel as Good News nowadays because people have become accustomed to understanding it in terms of the catechism and religious textbooks. The surprising novelty of the Gospel is hidden, enmeshed in formulas that no longer relate to the experience of ordinary people. This essay is not an attempt to give a new view on the Christian faith but to make the Good News live. To do that, it is necessary to disentangle the message from established patterns of religious terminology which no longer communicate the message, but instead make it obscure. Intended to be used in adult education and by religion teachers, this book does not aim to present a complete formulation of Christian faith. It aims, rather, to help the reader realize how meaningful Christian experience can be in today's world. The hope of the author is that, through its global approach, this essay will communicate the faith experience in a way that the traditional academic theology does not. It is also the author's belief that theology itself only progresses when ordinary people can confidently express their faith in a language which is their own and which is relevant to their contemporaries. Since this book is more concerned with the proclamation of the Good News than with its systematic organization, it could be said that it deals with "kerygmatic" theology, a language which makes the Gospel alive today.

The book is divided into three parts. The first part presents the Good News of Jesus Christ from a perspective which challenges some cultural assumptions of the past several hundred years; it can be considered an essay in itself. In the second part, some traditional theological concepts will be considered to see how they make sense once the underlying experience is understood. In the third part, we will examine modern philosophical and ideological concepts and how they can be relevant for theology today. This book, then, speaks of the same Good News from three different angles. The chapters have been written so that they can be read separately, but each needs to be understood in the context provided by the whole book. To allow for each chapter to be read separately, no attempt has been made to avoid repetition. However, each time the same concept is treated from different points of view, different aspects of its meaning become more apparent. It is assumed that the Good News cannot be understood by logical and analytical explanation alone. It is rather like a symphony whose principal theme has to come back and forth in order to impregnate the listeners. Quotations from the Gospel are not used here to *prove* anything, but to acknowledge that particular statements of the Gospel came alive for the author when he considered particular topics.

No attempt has been made, then, to give a theoretically comprehensive statement of the Christian message. The only objective is to show how it can make sense in relation to the experience of people today. This book is by no means a treatise of theology or a systematic catechesis. It is intended for Christians — including marginal Christians, or "former Christians" — for whom religious language has sometimes become more of a hindrance than help. For such persons, before they can grasp the meaning of a Christian discourse, some unlearning has to be done by which they give up their previous understanding (or misunderstandings). For example, it can happen that when the word "sin" is used, it induces such an association with guilt feelings that it becomes almost impossible to use the word to explain what the Church has to say in relation to the mystery of evil. Thus, one has to be very careful while touching upon that topic. That is why I will sometimes use the language of contrast, saying, for example, "sin is not . . .; but sin is. . . ." It must be recognized that such an approach can be misleading if it is understood too rigidly. For example, when Jesus said that those who will enter his kingdom are not those who say, "Lord, Lord," his use of contrast should not be taken to mean that Jesus despised prayer. Similarly, if I say that faith is not an intellectual experience, but the experience of a global liberation, I obviously do not want to discount its intellectual component. There is wisdom in the caution offered by the theologian Paul Tillich, who recommended that people be wary of the word "only" — at least when it is used literally. Contrasts, then, should not be understood too rigidly. When taken in a flexible way, they can be very helpful but otherwise they just contribute to a further sclerosis of theological arteries.

When it seems to me that the language of classical theology is "trapped" in association with meanings that are different from what it ought to express, I try to avoid it. It is, indeed, the job of pastoral theology to find new words to express the message of Jesus. These new presentations cannot be mere translations of former ones because a change in language always involves some change in meaning. While it is true that new expressions may lose some of the meaning of previous ones, it can also happen that the change brings to light another facet of the Good News of Jesus. Here and there, I will briefly indicate ways that the language that I am using may be related to classic theological formulations, but in doing so, I do not intend to reduce the wealth of classic traditions to my present discourse. More often, I do not make these relationships explicit, in the interest of clarity and simplicity. In any case, when all the theological formulations which seek to express the Good News for contemporary cultures are considered, it becomes obvious that time will be needed before the meditation of the Church will be able to discern between fruitful and reductionist approaches. The approach taken in this book becomes clearer when one considers the field where good wheat and bad weeds grow together. Let us hope that we will not be like the servants who are so zealous to take away the weeds that they prevent the wheat from growing.

A good part of this book has already been published, but not in its present form. The first part comes mainly from the now unavailable paperback, *The Good News That makes People Free.* But that book — written more than 10 years ago — has been substantially revised because it centered too much on interpersonal relationships and did not emphasize enough the face that action in behalf of justice and participation in the transformation of the world are constitutive parts of the preaching of the gospel (cf. International Synod of Bishops, Vatican, 1971). Many other changes — including the elimination of the sexist language — have been made. Some other chapters have been published in various periodicals, generally in a different form. Chapters 10 and 18 originally appeared in the *New Blackfriars;* Chapter 14 in the *Pro Mundi Vita Bulletin;* Chapter 20 in *La Revve Nouvelle;* Chapter 22 in *Worship;* and Chapter 23 in *The Catholic World;* the prayer for peace in Chapter 16 has been published in *Sister's Today.*

I want to thank all those who have helped me through their suggestions and criticism, especially my colleagues and my students at the University of Namur, Belgium, and at La Salle University, Philadelphia, Pennsylvania. My special thanks to J. Ahern, J. Baufay, J. Berleur, L. Biallas, J. Borremans, E. Demers, B. DiTommaso, M. Dumonceaux, J. Elias, A.M. Gardiner, B. Hogan, F. Hottlet, K. Loreman, A. Lorent, B. Lutz, G. Polis, B. Radtke, P. Renard, R. Wonders Rhoades, M. Shachter, A. St. James, G. Thill, J.M. Van Cangh and R. Waelkens.

— **Gerard Fourez**

INTRODUCTION
Beyond the Sacral and the Positivist Approaches

The purpose of this essay is to illuminate some aspects of the Christian faith from a *particular* point of view. Its concern is with Christian experience with life as it is experienced by people who have sought to follow Jesus now and in the past, going back to what we can know about the experience of Jesus himself.

The point of view adopted here begins with this observation. Many who have had a Christian upbringing view religion in what I shall characterize as a "sacral" and "positivist" frame of reference. I wish to propose an alternate approach, which is neither sacral nor positivist.

When I use the term "sacral," I mean the tendency to divide reality into "sacred" and "profane" realms. According to this world view, most of life is lived in a "profane" realm but certain well-defined realities are considered "sacred" and dependent on a supernatural order. People with this perspective are always trying to determine exactly where the sphere of God is located. They insist that we need to recognize "supernatural" realities. Thus, if a phenomenon such as prayer is considered, it is asserted that *beyond* a psychological analysis of this phenomenon, one has to show that there is a dimension that is entirely *non*-psychological.

On the contrary, the non-sacral point of view which I am going to present begins with the hypothesis that the ultimate dimension of our being is situated in a global reality within which there is no distincion between profane and sacred. For example, I shall not say that prayer is "something different from a psychological phenomenon"; but I shall propose that through a psychological phenomenon the ultimate human dimension is revealed, that is, the encounter with God. However, I shall avoid making use of propositions such as "Prayer is a purely psychological phenomenon," since such propositions with their insistence on the "purely" or on other similar logical operations (such as, "only through") suggest that the non-sacral point of view reduces everything to psychology or to some other rationally explicable phenomenon.

The non-sacral point of view that I am adopting is in no way meant to reduce reality to an impoverished meaning which would imply, for instance, that "humanity is nothing but psychology." I mean to say that it is in the global reality of humanity, this very reality that can be analyzed through natural sciences, social sciences, philosophy, or phenomenology, that the ultimate revelation of existence is finally found. This does not imply that there are no events, situations or individual persons where this global reality is being revealed more deeply. It simply means that God is revealed in creation, and not outside of it. Thus a non-sacral point of view asserts that it is in human, entirely human situations, that the Ultimate manifests itself. This actually is not different from the common teaching of Christian tradition that Jesus Christ is a human person who is the revelation of God, and that ultimate reality becomes incarnate: that is, that it manifests itself in *human* events.

The positivist point of view from which I will depart tends to value a "thing-oriented" (or "objectivist" or "materialist") view of reality. What interests the positivist is to place events in a scheme of interpretations supplied by the natural sciences: physics, chemistry, historical observation.

With this perspective, someone considering the statement that Jesus rose from the dead will immediately ask, "What happened to his body?" This positivist will wonder what happened inside the tomb Easter night and will be interested in what a journalist might write about it. If one talks about the Eucharist, the positivist's interest would seem to be a chemical one: "What is the difference between a loaf of bread before and after the consecration?"

The point of view which I propose suggests that such a degree of attention paid to the "positive" facts misses the essence of the Christian message. This essence has to do with the meaning of reality instead of merely with its observation. What happens, for example, in the eucharistic bread seems to me an altogether subordinate (and even a non-pertinent) question when one compares it to the meaning of the event, that is to the modifications of personal relations and of the significance of events which take place in the eucharistic celebration.

The ultimate dimension of our life is often concealed, then, by the sacral and positivist approach. It may also be obscured by a religious vocabulary that is outdated. My aim is to express that type of human experience to which the traditional Christian language actually refers, and thus to show that that language can introduce us to an experience of the ultimate dimension of life and the liberation of people. In other words, I shall try to discover the experiences to which Christians refer when they talk about revelation, salvation, rising from the dead, sacrament, gospel, God, Jesus, and other concepts which are part of the language of the Christian message.

DISCUSSION QUESTIONS

The following questions are intended to spark dialogue — of readers with the material in each chapter, of discussion groups of many kinds with one another and with this material. For the sake of clarity and to provide common ground for discussion, many questions simply ask how the reader has understood the main points in each chapter. Many questions therefore assume the framework of the interpretation presented in this book, and the phrasing of the questions may seem to imply that the "right" answers correspond with the positions taken in this book. The author wants to emphasize that this book offers only one interpretation (among many others that are possible) of the good news of God's love that comes to us in Jesus Christ; he thus invites readers and discussion groups to formulate their own further questions and interpretations.

N.B. If you have difficulty in handling any of the questions on the introduction, remember that it can be dropped.
1. In regard to *prayer,* what is the difference between a "sacral" approach and a "non-sacral" approach?
2. Is it true that if you do not take the "sacral" approach nothing is sacred anymore?
3. Take the statement: "God created the earth," and explain how it could be understood from a sacral approach, and from a non-sacral one. Do the same with the statement: "Jesus has risen from the dead."
4. Is it true that, in a non-sacral approach, people do not believe in the historicity of the resurrection?

PART 1
An Essay On Christian Experience

1
THE NOTION OF REVELATION

When speaking about Christian faith one speaks of course about "revelation." This term is misleading when it is taken to mean information transmitted by God to people independently of the meeting of persons. Such a conception is actually contrary to a central point of the traditional presentation of the Christian faith: that revelation consists in meeting Jesus, a particular individual who lived in a family, among a people, in a particular society. This encounter continues to happen through the mediation of living communities in which theology recognizes the "mystical body of Christ."

Revelation as an Experience, not Knowledge

Let us then undertake a reversal of the revelation-as-information perspective by examining the notion of revelation from a broader perspective. We may be helped by drawing a comparison with what can be said about love and friendship of whatever nature they might be. It is a common experience to realize that we are revealed to ourselves through others — individuals or communities. This kind of revelation is not so much a question of knowledge (although a certain knowledge is obviously always part of such an event) but much more of an existential experience.

Love reveals a dimension of existence that one may have never suspected. An attempt may be made to explain what is revealed, but this verbal explanation cannot completely describe what is experienced. It is impossible, if not ridiculous, to try to describe precisely the content of the revelation present in love; however some persons having had similar experiences discover that they understand each other when they talk about love. This is also true for the Christian revelation. It is essentially a meeting, a personal and communal meeting, the experience of a person or of a group. Through this meeting the ultimate dimension of existence, the one which the Gospel calls "the Father," the one whom the philosophical tradition called "God," is gradually revealed. This is not primarily the revelation of certain information but rather the experience of salvation, of being saved; in contemporary language, the experience of being liberated.

When I speak of revelation as an encounter with Jesus, I obviously do not speak of the same kind of meeting as when we meet people. As will be explained later, Jesus is not met through a kind of inner experience but through the Gospels and through people who seek to follow him by what they do as well as by what they say.

Revelation as Liberation

The notion of salvation as "liberation" is essential to the Christian faith which seeks a global liberation of all people in all dimensions of their lives. Every person is called to live according to the Beatitudes and, therefore, to be delivered from every yoke of oppression. Such yokes of oppression may result from political, social, economic, cultural or religious structures which exert a non-liberating force through external means or through their internalization in people. This is why this liberation cannot be "purely spiritual"; it has a social and hence a political dimension.[1]

Liberation takes place through the meeting of concrete persons and groups who live as Jesus did. Here it is essential to avoid abstract reasoning about the relationship of these persons to Jesus. It simply happens that in our present world there are people who say by their lives, "Listen! We have experienced liberation and at the same time the possibility of the liberation of all persons." Some who have had this experience explicitly name Jesus and Christian communities as the source of their liberation.[2] These people communicate a further message: "We have met the very Jesus whom the first Christian communities have presented in the Gospels. We have discovered that the Good News presented by these Christian communities has a meaning for us. Hence, we join the community of those who bear witness to his influence in human life and who continue his work of liberation."

This can happen in many ways. For some, the revelation of God's love will happen in their families; for others, it will occur through the encounter of caring Christians; it can also happen through the social involvement of Christians or through many other experiences. But for all those to whom Christian liberation is real, it is a revelation of a new and previously unimagined existence that comes to them through some Christian community. This liberation is not primarily a feeling, but a real event in the life of an individual, of a community and of a society.

To open ourselves to the Christian revelation, therefore, the essential thing is not adhering to an intellectual message but in being a part of a community that acknowledges a communion with the liberation of Jesus. Thus it does not so much matter to demonstrate to someone that "the Christian faith is true" as to work for the liberation of all. In addition, it may happen that, somehow through and thanks to this liberation, others will come into communion with the community of those who are liberated through Jesus and are thus in communion with the ever living Christ in the community. Consequently, to preach the Gospel is not to convert people to some sociologically identifiable group which purports to be the community of the faithful, but rather to labor in bringing to all, through action and not only through words, the Good News of liberation. That is how the community of the faithful is built as a social body.

This leads us to a clarification of the concept of faith. As the Christian tradition has always emphatically held, faith cannot be reduced to a belief in a set of doctrines. It is first an encounter with the very Spirit of God in Christians, and it is then a free acceptance of this Spirit and of the liberating actions that the Spirit instigates; and only finally it is adhering to some discourse expressing the faith. To receive faith, then, does not mean adhering to some truth; but rather, it implies changing the way a person or a community lives. The experience of faith is one through which we discover that we are not obliged, like the camel of which Nietzsche wrote, to bear the heavy load of doing the right thing and of believing the correct doctrine. On the contrary, the experience of faith enables us to accept being created and loved for our own sake. Such an experience, deeply associated with the discovery of being loved and of being liberated from every kind of oppression, is not a rational one. No good reason can be invoked for being so created out of love. It is utterly a gift which enables a person to be free.

In the following chapter we will try to characterize this change of perspective without which the Good News of liberation cannot be understood.

DISCUSSION QUESTIONS

1. Give some examples of "revealing" experiences in ordinary life.

2. Take some passages from the Gospel and show how they can be "revealing".

3. How would you explain a sacral and a non-sacral view of revelation?

4. What is the difference between looking at revelation as pure knowledge, and seeing revelation as an experience?

5. Explain the statement: "Revelation is not only a rational experience."

[1]That is why the bishops declared in 1971 at their International Synod in the Vatican: "Action on behalf of justice and participation in the transformation of the world fully appear to us as a constituative dimension of the preaching of the Gospel, or, in other words, of the Church's mission for the redemption of the human race and its liberation from every oppressive situation."

[2]Some people affirm that they have been liberated in Jesus Christ. This does not exclude the reality that it is possible to experience liberation without any explicit religious faith.

2
THE LIBERATION: JUSTIFICATION THROUGH FAITH OR JUSTIFICATION THROUGH WORKS

One of the major concerns of all of us is how to justify our lives, how to know what it is that ultimately gives our lives value for ourselves and possibly for others. In other words, it is essential for us to know whether we are worthy of existing in our own eyes and in the eyes of others. We often have a certain fear in this respect, asking ourselves to what degree we are worthwhile or lovable.

In this essay the expression, "A person is justified," will be used to indicate that we no longer need to prove ourselves either to ourselves or to others. Similarly, I shall say that we are lovable when we are able to accept love; that is, when we can accept being loved without immediately believing the one loving us is making a mistake. To say that we are lovable (love-able) does not mean that there are qualities in us for which we should be loved. As it will be emphasized later, we find ourselves lovable simply because somebody *does* love us, and not for any other particular reason. And moreover, when loved, we can experience self-worth.

When I speak of being "lovable," I do not seek academic answers to questions such as these: "Is everyone lovable?" or "Has each person a right to be loved?" It is obvious that love is a kind of basic need just as one needs food or shelter. Nowadays, it is commonplace to stress that everyone needs love and is by nature or by right "lovable." The Christian tradition speaks to this reality by asserting that even if we feel rejected by everyone, God loves us. But these statements can be very theoretical and unreal, just as, for example, the statement "all human beings are equal" is unreal if we do not recognize the inequalities in any actual society with its accumulated history of injustices and unjust structures. This "lovableness" is not experienced as a datum of nature but as a liberating experience; and that experience only happens when someone is really loved. Outside of actual love — which, beyond the relational dimension, also implies a cultural, political, and economic one — lovableness is only a word, as equality is only a word outside actual civil rights and just economic structures. That is also why the lovableness of everyone is only a datum in hope and something yet to be done. Indeed, we will see that it is the Christian mission.

One may say that people who know that they really are "lovable" are "justified." In order to better understand this point, let us consider the example of lovers. One could say that if they find it is acceptable (natural?) to be loved and accept this fact easily, they are justified. They are lovable, and they believe that they are, as a consequence of being loved — not only in words but also in deeds. In accepting love and rejoicing at being loved, they experience their justification. But if they feel unworthy of being loved to the point of feeling uneasy, and if they have the impression of not being basically lovable, one could say they are not "justified." The problem of justificatioin is thus the essential problem of a human being: Does my being there make a difference to anyone, to humankind, or to the world? Am I lovable? Is my existence justifiable?

Two Very Different Attitudes

People attempt to be justified in different ways. Basically, there are two opposite ways of facing this question. For some, justification comes from what they will *do* in order to become "acceptable" and "lovable." Others, on the contrary, will consider themselves justified not by what they do, but because they trust that others accept and love them. They believe that love is given freely. It is not earned. It will not be withdrawn. It does not carry a price tag, although its demands are felt. These two attitudes are entirely different. One could say that the first group seeks to be justified through their works, while the others seek to be justified by their faith, that is, by their trust in others. By contrast, in our industrial and post-industrial society, people are conditioned to seek their justification in their works or in the "right" appearance.

The choice of one or the other of these attitudes makes a considerable difference in one's way of life. Let us consider once more the example of the lovers. Those who want to be justified through works are busy with some kind of Sisyphean labor[1] which will never be finished. Each time they achieve something, they come to the conclusion that, whatever they have done does not yet justify being loved. Hence they will always have to do more and yet will never attain their end. When people feel that they have to *prove* themselves worthy of love, they will inevitably come to the conclusion that they are not lovable. Unfortunately, many have been conditioned to feel that way. There are many persons who try to prove in one way or another that they are lovable, but who do not really believe it themselves. Psychologists know them well; they approach others paralyzed with fear of themselves, sure that they are worth nothing and without any real hope with regard to their own lives.

Altogether different is the attitude of those who, knowing well that they are not at all *worthy* of being loved, are nonetheless not anxious, since they *know* they are loved. They are confident in the fact that someone really loves them, and this actions that they are worthy of the love being given to them.

And at the same time they know they are loved for themselves, for what they are and because of their worthiness. Love recognizes and reveals someone's value (Cf. the chapter on grace, Part II, Chapter 11).

These persons know well their alienations, contradictions, limitations, and their basic helplessness; they feel justified not through their works, but through trust and faith. It should be pointed out that they will be just as efficient in action as those who always want to achieve something to justify themselves. But the former do not act *in order to* justify themselves; on the contrary, it is *because* they know they are loved that they feel capable of doing much and thus of sharing their experience of love. Being loved before they were aware of their need for love, they are awakened to the possibilities of their lives. This love that comes unbidden saves them from the temptation of despairing, inherent in the human situation because one fears that one's life will come to nothing.

There is then a fundamental difference between those who base their lives on a justification through works and those who rely on justification through faith. For the former, to be acceptable and lovable is the consequence of their works. For the latter, their works are the consequence of their being loved and accepted. They can recognize their own value and dignity because they have been accepted and loved by others. But a question arises: "How does a person crushed by societal or interpersonal oppression come to trust enough to believe in love?"

Justification as Liberation

If I am engaged in that Sisyphean labor of justification through works, it is not easy to accept justification through faith. To pass from one framework to another, an experience of liberation is necessary. Liberation is an experience by which I realize in a personal way that I am loved and am thus enabled to act out of this realization. I am freed from the burden of proving or of "justifying" myself.

Since liberation is an experiential realization, it always occurs in a social environment through particular individuals and groups. And since people do not live alone, liberation is possible only if certain social and collective conditions are satisfied. It is *impossible* for someone to be entirely liberated in alienating structures. The racist, sexist, exploitative, dictatorial, or imperialist structures of our world oppress people both internally, because of the way people come to view themselves and the world, and externally in the lack of real opportunities available to many people. Since we exist in such structures, liberation is always incomplete. And so the promotion of liberation demands a complete restructuring of life, at the personal as well as at the collective level. The ultimate aim of the Christian mission is that the love of God be made visible in the individual and collective conditions of humanity. That is why total liberation is not a given; it remains, as we will emphasize later, a mission to be accomplished in history. That is also why the 1971 International Synod of Bishops stressed that action in behalf of justice and participation in the transformation of the world is a constitutive part of the preaching of the Good News.

The liberation, the realization of the Good News, is the awareness that I am loved and accepted independently of what I do. This is what the evangelist John means when he says that God has loved us first, while we were still sinners. To be a Christian then is to be liberated by trust, to have a concrete experience of the love of God which affects us to the point that we understand that we need not rely upon works in order to be loved by God. (Obviously, this love of God reaches us through people.) There is no *need* to work for our justification, since we are justified through God's love. Works then spring from this experience; they do not cause it. We are justified free of charge, "by grace," through the gratuitous love of God and of others. (But, obviously, we generally experience this love of God only through the actual love of people who transform both our relationships and our society.)

Thus the Christian experience, as it is described by the theology of justification through faith, can be expressed more or less in the following terms: God loves us and that love affects us through the love of those persons who make this love of God concrete and obvious to us. This justifies us, releases us from *having to prove* that we are lovable, and helps us to be ourselves. As a consequence we are able to act, not to justify ourselves, but *because* we are justified. But in order for all this to be a reality and not just a comforting dream, this love of God must be made visible, in a concrete way, in the individual and collective living conditions of humanity; liberation is not only an internal or spiritual experience, it has societal dimensions.

Justification, Ethics, and Grace

It is with this understanding that one can comprehend the nature of Christian ethics. It is not a condition for justification or of salvation. People who discover themselves being loved rejoice in the freedom[2] opened to them and strive to be present to others, to participate in the world in a way that is consonant with their experience of being liberated. Thus the action of Christians is called to be part of the history of the struggle of all creation for liberation. That is Christian ethics: a result rather than a cause of God's liberating love. Christians are called upon to be persons and groups believing and trusting in a coming liberation which will set right the unjust structures of society. The Christian ethic is thus a call for action in behalf of God's reign of love and its justice.

Thus a complete reversal of perspective must be made in regard to certain concepts. If the Christian is liberated by faith and not through works, the guilt complexes of a certain type of Catholic moralism lose their meaning. People can utterly trust themselves. The reason for this confidence is that God loves people and, therefore, justifies them. The result of God's love is the confidence of people in themselves. Moreover, if we become conscious of this confidence in ourselves, we also know that this trust and this justification come from others and from God. We are like the lovers who know perfectly well that love makes us strong and that, while originating in the one who loves us, this force is our own. Hence the dependence of humanity in God is not one in which we are obliged to do something for the other, but an extremely liberating experience in which, loved by the other, we are truly free to be ourselves thanks to this love.

This is "justification by grace," that is, by the gracious love of God. A Christian perspective affirms that it is the gracious love of God which makes people free and able to be themselves, independently of all the works they may accomplish for this purpose. God does not measure, but gives gratuitously.

If one understands that the Christian is in this way justified by faith, one realizes the ambiguity of the familiar assertion that humanity has been created *for* God. People are not created for God, since God loves them and therefore wants them to belong to themselves. To regard seriously the traditional doctrines of creation through love is to believe that humanity has a value of its own because God loves every human person. To claim to be a believer in the Christian God, thus, means to use a symbolic language that expresses a faith that the ultimate meaning of existence is an absolute gift despite every closure and measure of life. It implies living in a new way in a human history where there is evil. That was essential to the life of this amazing man Jesus who is at the base of the Christian faith. He is the living revelation of what God's love is.

DISCUSSION QUESTIONS

1. In this chapter, what is the understanding of "being justified"?

2. Can the experience of being liberated be solely an individual experience? Why not?

3. How would you characterize "justification by faith"? "justification by works"?

4. What is the connection between justification by works and the so-called puritan ethic?

5. Relate the experience of justification by faith to the experience of gratuitousness.

6. Find some examples of Gospel stories which obviously are rooted in a justification-by-faith experience.

7. Why is justification by works very much like a curse?

8. Explain how a person can come to believe in justification by faith.

9. What is the connection between justification by faith and the need for socio-political action?

10. If you consider a love relationship, what would it mean to live it in a "justification-by-works" or in a "justification-by-faith" perspective?

11. Comment on the statement: "We should try hard to get to the 'justification by faith' level."

12. Does "justification by faith" mean that we will stop acting to improve society? How does justification by faith relate to action?

13. Considering a juvenile delinquent, how does "justification by faith" and "by works" speak to his or her condition?

14. "Law and order" people are sometimes afraid of "justification by faith". Why? Was that already evident in Jesus' time?

---

[1]In Greek mythology, Sisyphus was forced to push a rock up a mountainside. Before he could reach the top, the rock would roll back down, and he was doomed to repeat the process interminably.

[2]The concept of freedom is difficult to define; perhaps one of the most appropriate ways is to say that freedom is a situation where people do not have to fear, can truly say what they want and are able to live in peace through the unavoidable conflicts of life. Such a freedom is the result of love as John says: "Perfect love casts away fear." (I John 4:18) Actually freedom is a mythical or utopian concept; we only experience partial liberations. Likewise, we cannot have an absolute, comprehensive concept of freedom. The Hebrew concept "shalom" could, however, be an appropriate representation of what we mean by liberation.

3
WHO IS JESUS?

In order to understand who Jesus is, I shall present a brief account of the Gospel of Mark from a very particular point of view. Mark's version introduces itself as the "Good News about Jesus Christ, the Son of God" (1:1). He first relates how Jesus discovers at his baptism that the Spirit of the Father is upon him; he is told: "You are my Son, the Beloved; my favor rests on you" (1:11). Moved and strengthened by this experience, Jesus presents himself to his people and the Good News is announced (1:15). Jesus' experience of discovering that he is really loved by the one whom he comes to call Father is fundamental to an understanding of his life. Because Jesus trusts that he is loved, he is able to do wonderful deeds to make "real" the good news of the love of God.

Mark tells how, immediately after that experience, Jesus confronts evil in the desert. Jesus' awareness of being loved by his Father is connected with a confrontation with evil which Mark makes explicit in chapters 1:22-3:6. That section of his Gospel could be called the Gospel of the transgressions. It shows Jesus confronting many oppressions which afflicted people. To respond to the needs of people, Jesus transgresses various laws and taboos, daring to speak and act with authority, thus bringing the Good News of liberation in word and deed. This will finally lead him to a serious confrontation with the Pharisees on the Sabbath Day in the synagogue (3:1-6). After that incident, the Pharisees enter into an alliance with the members of

24

Herod's party for the purpose of killing Jesus. The meaning of the whole life of Jesus is summarized when his liberating freedom leads him to confront the powerful of this world and, in the end, to face execution. But to understand that story, is to believe in the Good News of a God who does not measure and whose reign is at hand and so to change our mentality. The Gospel thus invites people to a "metanoia," that is, to a total change in their way of looking at everything, including laws, purity, sin, authority, power, transgression, and various groups of people. This change of heart is exemplified in Jesus' deeds.

The Power Given to People

This Good News appears in a series of rather unusual events. Jesus dares to teach with authority (not like the scribes and the Pharisees) (1:22) and to be free; he refuses to be bound by a stereotyped image such as the Holy One of God (1:24). He dominates situations involving unclean spirits; he has confidence in himself and they obey him (1:27). In reading this Gospel, one is impressed by the clear affirmation of human freedom (Matthew 9:8). This self-confidence of Jesus is the sign of the liberation coming from God, since it is a confidence in the love of God for man. The episode of the paralytic (2:9) is rather typical. Jesus is not afraid to forgive his sins (2:10). Linked to this event is the invitation Jesus will address to people to mutually forgive one another's sins. (Eventually the power of Jesus will belong to every person, and this will be apparent in his/her using that power to forgive each other.) Being enabled to offer pardon is of major importance, and being so empowered is very liberating because people are always conscious of their limitations.

As Jesus continues to act he becomes no less disconcerting. He does not withdraw from sinners, those whom he has come to summon and to liberate (2:15). Even fasting, so central to the preaching of John the Baptizer, becomes secondary (2:18). One has to change one's attitude decisively and to move away from the ancient vision of the world in which humanity felt itself to be inescapably sinful, unwelcome and incapable of self-confidence. One should not attempt to put this new wine into old wineskins; for new wine, one really needs fresh skins (2:22). The power which is revealed in Jesus is such that the ancient religious taboos are turned upside down. The Son of Man and, finally, all persons are masters of the Sabbath (2:27).

A first reading of this section of Mark's gospel might give an impression of Jesus as a person who dares to be and to speak. But, in itself, such a reading would be too individualistic and has to be completed.[1] It can also be shown how, because of the Good News, Jesus confronts every kind of oppression that crushes people and so reveals the justice of God's kingdom. That brings to him some allies and some adversaries. Through these conflicts he is led to choose his solidarities and to struggle against his enemies. Jesus takes the part of a people oppressed by innumerable rules defining what was pure and what was impure (1:23), by the fear of saying something not written in the book (1:27), by many kinds of disease (1:34), by demonic possession (1:34), by a lack of forgiveness (2:5), by prescriptions related to fasting (2:18), by society's rejection of sinners and publicans (2:15), and by the Sabbath law (2:23). These norms are transgressed by Jesus for the sake of a liberation, a salvation. And so Jesus becomes a subversive person, threatening the established order of society, at least when it crushes people.[2] Ordinary people, when they see the stands that Jesus takes, praise God and rejoice; the Pharisees and the Scribes, however, begin to be upset; and so Jesus moves to gather a group of disciples to proclaim the Good News. The underlying conflict is clearly revealed in the solemn transgression at the beginning of chapter 3. There Mark describes how the Pharisees and the Scribes confront Jesus to see if he dares to challenge the established order in the synagogue on the Sabbath day. In that context, Jesus asks the man with the withered hand to stand up in front of the assembly. He then asks whether or not it is permitted to do good on the Sabbath. While the Pharisees remain silent, Jesus, filled with anger and sorrow, cures the man and so challenges the establishment. From this moment the powerful decide to kill him (3:6). Jesus is not — as some seem to believe — a peaceful person who always agrees with everybody. On the contrary, in a society characterized by oppressive structures, Jesus chooses his solidarities and his friends, recognizing that as a consequence of his stands, he is the enemy of the powerful.

Faced with such a prophet, the crowd comes from everywhere (3:7). His liberating power flows from the reality that Jesus himself is free because of his experience of the love of his father. But that power is not a privilege for himself alone. The freedom to "do on the Sabbath" is meant for everyone. Those who believe in the gift of God will be able to act as Jesus did, and to perform even greater deeds. Jesus thus reveals what we become when we believe in the gift of God, that is, when we believe in ourselves, since that is exactly what a human being is: the gift of God. This message goes beyond Israel and reaches the country of Tyre and Sidon (3:8). Jesus' Good News thus helps people to stand up as persons, but it also threatens oppressive structures and the position of the powerful of this world.

For those who do not believe, Jesus is judged a strange person. He appears to have taken leave of his senses, to be possessed by evil spirits (3:22). In this way, various people express their judgment that the liberty he seems to enjoy is unacceptable to them. He pushes his message further and further. In the face of a society where mistakes were counted, he asserts that pardon is total (3:28).[3] He reveals further that people are liberated from social structures that are too narrow; to those who point out his mother and his brothers, Jesus affirms that everyone can be his brother and sister (3:35). In so opening the too narrow universe of the family, he obviously threatens the family organization and he challenges the established order by questioning classic social roles. The liberation offered in Jesus, though held out to all, does not bear fruit everywhere, as we hear in the parable of the sower (4:1). However, the same parable tells us that where the Good News is welcomed, there are fruits so amazing that they are beyond the normal (4:8). Every parable of the Kingdom tends to express how very important the fruits of liberation are. The parable of the lamp points out that whoever is liberated can live in full daylight (4:22). The parable of the measures shows that there is no limit to the gift of God, to the liberation God brings. Mark's Gospel describes surprise at seeing a seed, which should have produced only a vegetable, become a tall tree; such is the person who believes in his liberation (4:30).

However, since all this is said in parables, one does not understand it immediately (4:33). It is difficult for people to really believe in complete liberation. They tend to return to their bondage and to a life limited by social and religious conventions which impede the full blossoming of liberation. And we will see that social structures will try to bring them back to the established disorder.

Because he is liberated, Jesus is not anxious about perishing in the storm. He asks, "Why are you so frightened? How is it that you have no faith?" (4:40). The person whose faith is complete no longer needs to fear. This does not mean that there is nothing to fear, but that to have faith and to be liberated means to live with fear tamed by trust in life, even when facing the eventuality of death. This is the Good News of liberation for us: that even death can be faced with trust. Mark then insists that salvation may reach everyone, even those living outside Israel (the "heathen"), and those possessed by a legion of evil spirits (5:1). The customary boundaries have no meaning in relation to salvation. No one is given preference as is seen when the synagogue official's request for the cure of his daughter is heard only after the woman with the hemorrhage is healed (5:35). There is no priority in entering the Kingdom. One is saved simply *because of one's faith and one's trust.*

The opposition between the free person who is Jesus and the

community in which he was born becomes more and more real. The inhabitants of Nazareth cannot accept him, and he is, therefore, unable to liberate them (6:5). He nevertheless sends his disciples everywhere insisting that they need have no fear, that they, too, can speak with authority (6:10).

The Intolerable Person?

In conclusion, let us briefly touch upon other episodes related by Mark. We see the compassion of Jesus toward the crowd (6:34); his ordering the disciples to give *themselves* something to eat (6:37); the liberating message that nothing is unclean, but that it is only from within, from the heart, that evil intentions emerge, and uncleanness is created (7:21); and the denunciation of pharisaical hypocrisy (7:12). All this leads to the moment when Peter recognizes in Jesus the Messiah, the Christ (8:29), the one who will change the people's fate.

At this time when he is acknowledged as having a dignity beyond anything that could be imagined, Jesus warns Peter that he must suffer and die (8:31). This coincidence does not seem to be a mere accident, and demands comment on the reasons for Jesus' death. It is often suggested that his death came almost in an arbitrary way through some strange decree of God. This God is a tyrant who sends his Son to suffer.

What actually caused the death of Jesus is the conflict inherent in his way of life. He presented himself as a person liberated by God, master of the Sabbath and friend of the rejected, having power over everything. That was too much; established society could not accept such a person. The elders, the scribes, the priests, that is, all the powerful and guardians of that unjust society seek to have him killed. As the grand inquisitor in Dostoyevsky's legend declares, such liberty has to be eliminated. And this is why his death looms up on the background at the moment he appears to be completely free in the opinion of people, at the moment he appears transfigured in the eyes of the apostles. The rest of the Gospel relates the inevitable approach of his end . . . such a person is not acceptable and must be eliminated (14:1). As the opera *Jesus Christ Superstar* says so adequately: "This Jesus must die." Jesus thus becomes a sign of contradiction. Peter persists in believing that the worst can be avoided (8:32) but Jesus realizes it is impossible for him to continue to stand for the reign of God and its justice, without being banned and rejected. The disciples find cause for fear (9:32) as they begin to realize how radically different from the world is the kingdom proclaimed by Jesus.

In the kingdom, the powerful become the last (9:35); the privileges of men with respect to women are deeply challenged (10:2-12), and it is easier for a camel to go through the eye of a needle than for a rich person to enter the kingdom (10:25). Finally, Jesus is rejected, given to the army of the occupying power by the chiefs of the people (10:33-34) and deserted, in the end, by crowds and disciples alike. The challenge of Jesus is found unacceptable and the guardians of the establishment finally defend themselves against it. Because he has taken on himself God's own struggle for justice in an unjust society, Jesus is executed. It is, therefore, not adequate just to say that Jesus accepts death out of love. Actually, he is killed in a very specific societal conflict, thus showing how God takes sides in history and in society. Jesus, as he dies, is seen as an outcast, crucified among the brigands, a scandal for those who believe that God is essentially found in power, beauty, or even in established religion.

A decisive question is how Jesus will react in the face of the acuteness of the conflict. At the last Supper, betrayed by a friend, Jesus finally decides to give his life for his people, even to the point of death (14:27). He does this out of trust and love for the one he calls his father.

Jesus does not die because of some strange sadistic God who had to be satisfied by another's suffering. Jesus dies because some people, having power, could not accept his kingdom of justice and decided to kill him. Confronted with that hatred and desiring to be faithful to his mission, Jesus could choose either to try to defend his way of life by every possible means or to accept being killed. Had he opted for the first alternative Jesus would have had to mobilize all his energy to defend himself; while doing that, he would have been just one more politician among many. He would not have been faithful to the spirit of love and freedom. When confronted with oppressors, he would have simply become one of them, using the same means and operating out of the same ideology.

That is why he knows that the hour will come when the only way in which he can remain free and faithful will be to be on the side of the oppressed and the powerless. Even if he is not against every kind of violence (e.g., 11:15-18) he realizes that it is not simply in countering a sword with a sword that people become free. As it is emphasized in *Jesus Christ Superstar,* he believes that neither the Pharisees nor the Romans, nor Simon the Zealot, nor the crowd understand what power is. He knows that power is only meaningful when one is ready to give it up. He knows that it can be painful for a human being to face such abandonment and such a death. It is a cup which is repulsive, and which people do not want to drink. But he knows that if he should cling so desperately to his life and his mission as to refuse to drink it, then his liberation will not be real. And that is why he also knows that such an acceptance of death is the only way. But when the hour comes, the only thing he will be aware of is the feeling of losing himself and everything.

That is the same feeling that many human beings have experienced when they realize that the only meaningful way for them is to trust to the point of feeling abandoned. And here is where the saving power of Jesus' death lies: rather than becoming an oppressor, he preferred, when the choice came to that, to share the fate of the oppressed. Jesus' liberation and the way in which he is related to others is such that he can face death for his people (14:24). Here again, one need not imagine some magic force in the act of dying for someone else or in the idea that God would be appeased by this oblation. It is much more deeply human. Jesus knows that one cannot promote the kingdom of forgiveness and the freedom of others by intruding but only in making oneself vulnerable. And it is through that process that the glory of God is manifested. The Last Supper and the Passion proclaim that vulnerability which is truly liberating, both for the person who makes the decision to be vulnerable and for others.

To be free implies not to be moved by fear (which is always present), particularly by fear of death. The free person is therefore vulnerable, and it is to be expected that destruction will come. Because he decided to be "for others," the only attitude Jesus may have towards those who want to eliminate him is silence. There is no more time to argue or to defend himself. Before "his hour" Jesus could dispute and dismiss the Pharisees. At the moment of his Passion, such a debate would have served no purpose but to hide what really happened: the rejection of the liberated person who was Jesus and of his justice in this society. That is why, at that moment, the faithful love of Jesus for his people brought him to give his life for them. And that is why, following Jesus, and in memory of him, many people, also struggling for justice, will also say: "Here is my life for you."

The Death of Jesus and God's Solidarity

Some fifteen years ago, the emphasis in theology was less and less on the death of Jesus, as many Christians began to stress the resurrection. This tendency to "erase" the death of Jesus reflected a mind set which believed that modern progress in its many forms was on the verge of solving all the problems of humankind. Christians today, more conscious of death and oppression on earth, are turning again to wonder why Jesus died. In South America and in countries where Christians frequently risk their lives for human liberation, this question of the death of Jesus is particularly meaningful.[4]

The first Christians were deeply disturbed by the torture and execution of Jesus, which they experienced as a scandal or a meaningless event. Rather quickly, the designation of Jesus as the "suffering servant of Yaweh" was put aside; people felt more at ease with titles that referred more to the resurrection, such as Messiah, Lord, Son of God, Logos, and so forth. The cross was increasingly seen only as a preliminary step leading toward resurrection. Another way of minimizing the cross was to provide "logical" explanations for Jesus' death. So the scandal of his execution and torture was more or less replaced by theories explaining "why it had to be like that," according to God's plan. These explanations, yesterday as today, end in concealing existential and societal conflicts. They tell us that God loves us, but they do not consider *how* God has manifested love and salvation. Thus, they give us an image of God independent of the death of Jesus on the cross, and a cultic notion of sacrifice that does not stem from the Gospel or from the surrender of Jesus in Golgotha. Theologies which show the Father as wanting Jesus' death in expiation for sins not only represent God as a sadistic person, but also conceal the historical and concrete reasons why Jesus was rejected by people. A Greek and metaphysical concept of God as a perfect and extratemporeal being completes the concealment of the conflicts at the background of Jesus' death.

On the contrary, a theologian like Sobrino suggests that a truly historical liberation theology sees suffering as a way of being that which belongs to God. And the cross then appears as the result of the incarnation in a sinful world which acts as a power fighting against the God of Jesus. Thus, Jesus died because he lived to the end the conflict resulting from his witness to the reign of God in a society that wanted another God than the merciful and just God of Jesus. If Jesus has been condemned as a subversive person, it is not because his story can be reduced to a political power struggle, but because his love was finally political and not merely idealistic; his love was

real and concrete in an actual historical situation. And if Jesus
was condemned as a blasphemer, it happened because his God
was very different from the God of his judges. Thus the conflict
that leads to Jesus' death concerns much more than a merely
inner or mystical salvation; it is the end result of a historical
life in a specific society. That is why Christian spirituality
cannot be reduced to an idealistic mystique of the cross, but
means following the historical path of Jesus.

These are the reasons why Jesus' execution raises questions
with respect to the places where his God is today. Jesus was
crucified among outcasts. This is the scandal of the cross. This
challenges Christian communities when they seek to be in solidarity with the establishment. It is surely more appealing to
envision a risen Christ who is imagined beyond all the conflicts
that divide society, and who could never be dreamed of as a marginal person. People are thus often tempted to elaborate
theologies explaining Jesus' death without being challenged to
see the many ways in which he is put to death in our contemporary society. On the contrary, when people accept being confronted with Jesus' execution, they are led to consider all those
that the established order (or disorder) crushes, and, therefore,
to consider the socio-political dimension of the sin of the world.
Questions arise: "Are those who call themselves Christians in
solidarity with the one who has been killed? What does it mean
to be in solidarity with Jesus, in our present society? What
does it mean to trust God as he did?" According to such a
theology, Jesus' death is central in the Christian faith because
it sends Christians toward the historical tensions in which they
have to take a stand. It reveals that it is in these tensions —
and not in the clouds — that people can discern who God is
and who is Jesus' God. Jesus' execution raises, with the serious-
ness of death, a simple question: "With whom are we in solidarity? With whom is God in solidarity?"

Mark ends his Gospel with the discovery of the empty tomb.
Confronting us with this experience of an ever-living Christ for

whom certain people bear witness, Mark invited us to take a position (16:8). The "community of the faithful" will be the assembly, the Church, of those who by following the ever living Christ have decided to be vulnerable, to be in solidarity with the poor and the oppressed, to struggle for the Kingdom and its justice, and thus to bring the Good News to people.

DISCUSSION QUESTIONS

1. Do you feel some differences of perspective between the way you usually read the Gospel and this kind of interpretation?

2. Find some Gospel passages which make more sense if you do not project on them an immediate understanding of the post-Resurrection belief that Jesus is God.

3. Comment on the "authority" of Jesus, and relate it to your understanding of the "authority of the people."

4. In which experience is the authority of Jesus grounded?

5. Why was Jesus unacceptable to those in power in his society?

6. In this interpretation of Jesus' life, why is he executed? Compare different views of Jesus' death.

7. Why is the last supper an important moment in Jesus' life?

8. If you say that Jesus was killed because of his stands with respect to societal issues, does that take something away from the statement: "He died out of love for his father and for his people"?

9. How can one interpretation of Jesus' death lead to a privatized religion, and another to a socially committed one?

---

[1]A reading that takes into account the societal conflicts which are part of Jesus' life brings some hermeneutical questions. Two stumbling blocks have

to be avoided. The first would be a reading which projects into Jesus' society tensions from our own historical situation. The other, however, would be a way of looking at Jesus' life without noticing that some conflicts are very similar to those that we call "class-conflicts." The way in which Jesus behaves in these conflicts challenges our own social practices without offering us any pat answers for our social problems which cannot be precisely the same as those which faced Jesus in his society.

[2]Jesus, however, does not transgress just for the sake of transgressing, but to liberate people, groups, and mentalities. When the law does not impose some useless yoke — as when it requests the cured lepers to show themselves to the priest — Jesus accepts and affirms it. In the Christian tradition, any kind of establishment — such as power, institutions, family, law — is seen as the gift of God as well as one of the places where the historical sin of the world is expressed.

[3]Except if one sins against the Spirit. To sin against the Spirit, I believe, is the refusal to accept that God grants his gift. St. Paul would say that this means the refusal to be saved by grace, that is, by the gracious love of God.

[4]Cf the Book of Jon Sobrino: *Christology at the Crossroad* (Orbis Books, Maryknoll, 1977). Many of the following considerations were inspired by this work of a South American liberation theologian.

4
THE MISSION OF THE CHURCH: A MISSION OF LIBERATION

Facing the limits of the institutional church and the postconciliar challenges, we are bound to ask a fundamental question: "What, after all, is the mission of the Church?" The purpose of this chapter is to point out and explain that its mission is the liberation of people. This liberation is not simply a personal, even less only a spiritual one; it is global and must encompass action on behalf of justice and the historical transformation of the world. That is how the church will manifest the love and the power of God.

What is the Good News?

When John the Baptist sent some of his disciples to question Christ and to ask him whether it was he who was promised to come, the answer was clear: "Go back and tell John what you have seen and heard: the blind see again, the lame walk, lepers are cleansed, the deaf hear, the dead are raised to life and the Good News is proclaimed to the poor." The message is clear: Jesus shows through these signs that the Kingdom has come; these signs announce liberation for the people. The whole gospel and the life of Jesus is just that: a way of living this liberation.

Liberated people are above the law; they can live, forgive, decide for themselves without fear; they can face even death. Such is the Good News: a liberation announced on behalf of God's love. Of course, this liberation always has to be accomplished, both on the personal and on the social level. It is not possible to reach that freedom in an oppressing or exploitative society.

This concept of the Good News is somewhat ambiguous. It has two dimensions: an *announcement* of liberation intended by God and brought by Jesus and the *actions* that realize that liberation. If one understands that the Good News is an announcement of liberation, bringing the Good News will consist in transmitting the Message: "God loves you, and his love liberates you." But if the Good News consists in the effecting of liberation, bringing the Good News means to truly set persons and groups free by making the love of God manifest through human love in the relational as well as in societal structures of history. This emphasis on the actual manifestation of the liberating love of God goes, for Christians, with the memory and the witness of its revelation in Jesus.

From the gospel I believe there is just one possible answer: the Good News is not simply an intellectual message, not only information, but mainly a reality which has to be made actual: people being liberated. Even more, the message of the Good News gets its value and meaning only because of the liberation it effects. A paradigm of that liberation is Zacchaeus who, because Jesus accepted him, truly became free. The very way he behaved after having met Jesus actually indicates what freedom brings: action on behalf of justice.

That experience of Zacchaeus can take many forms in our contemporary world. It can be the discovery by a man who is a migrant worker of some organized group or union where he may truly be himself; or for a woman who is an alcoholic, the encounter with somebody who believes in her and trusts her; or in a more peaceful way, it may be the loving care of parents for their child. But in all cases the Good News will only be announced when it will have produced its effect, i.e., the actual liberation of people. To bring the Good News thus implies an action in our society as it is, that is, touched by all kind of historical evil.

To Bring the Good News

The coming of the Kingdom of God seems, therefore, to be structured as follows: Some persons and groups, through active love, do concretely liberate individuals and groups. Those who have discovered themselves liberated (in a more traditional language one would say, "saved") through a gratuitous love which has touched them form a community of faithful. That community is what is called the Church. In their turn these faithful also want to bring the Good News to others, since people will not be liberated if nobody takes these steps.[1] Thus to bring this Good News does not consist essentially in explaining a set of beliefs; rather it consists in acting in such a way that others too are loved and liberated. The fruit and the sign of this liberation is that individuals do exist beyond the limitations imposed by legal, social and psychological constraints because they are loved.[2] In the traditional formula, one would say, they are saved by grace, that is, by a gracious love. To be complete, this liberation can obviously not be limited to individuals but has to be concerned with society as a whole. It cannot consist solely of ideas; it must be real. It should initiate change in the alienating structures of society. The Church, that is, the community of faithful, perceives that its mission is to celebrate its completely gratuitous liberation and to act for the liberation of people.

Thus the main mission of the Church is not to convey a message or a creed, but to accomplish a liberation. This is the reason why the Church ought normally to be ripe for revolution, that is, for a complete change of mentality, as well as of political and economic systems.

If the preceding point of view is accepted, there are some very concrete implications for the Church and for Christians. First, the Church needs a different style of mission. Very often indeed, Christians have separated belief and liberation to such an extent that the Good News often seems to simply boil down to a message: in our society, an individual is often called a Christian simply because of adherence to a creed. It would obviously be more gospel-like to recognize as a Christian the one who discovers himself liberated and who is therefore capable of behaving as a free person — someone like Zacchaeus.

On the contrary, when being a Christian appears to be an imposed burden or a programme to be accomplished, there is no liberation, and it has to be concluded that the Good News is not yet realized. Thus, it can be recognized that the Church is not always liberating and therefore often fails in its mission to bring the Good News.

Second, liberation should completely change the lives of people. Thus the community of the faithful needs to emphasize more strongly the deep (let us say "mystical") change that is implied by the advent of a person to "salvation," to liberation. Catholics would have much to learn from some Protestants who present the faith in this perspective. The test of the Good News is that it enables people to follow Jesus and so to face life, world and death in hope.

If we realize that we live in a context of psychosocial alienation from ourselves and each other (this is actually related to the traditional doctrine of original sin), it becomes obvious that the process of liberation also calls for a radical restructuring of society. Liberation will be incomplete as long as the social structures in which people live institutionalize the alienation between persons or groups of persons rather than give a communal social expression of the change in human relations that liberation implies for humankind.

The community of the faithful, which is the Church, is called to be a ferment of liberation for the whole society, first in the manner in which it structures its own relationships and secondly in the manner in which it influences the whole society. This is necessary so that humankind may yet live in a structure that does not impose the roles of oppressor-oppressed, superior-inferior, upper class-lower class, and so forth.

The first aspect, its own structural form, is most easily symbolized in the celebration of the Good News, the liturgy. In this action, the community recognizes that its source of liberation is the unconditional love of Jesus which creates them into a new social body where all the parts are equally important and respected. The second aspect, its impact on society, is what is often called its mission.

The Mission of the Church

The priority given to actual liberation entails consequences for the mission of the Church. It is inaccurate to present the Church as having to propagate the faith on one hand and to be active in society on the other. This duality is false. The mission of the Church is to bring the Good News, that is, to make actual the signs of God's love; this means therefore liberating and, through that liberation, announcing the gift and the love of God. In consequence, bringing the faith and liberating people are one.

And if there is nobody to bring this Good News, the people will not be freed. This is evidenced by the millions of those who are alienated, whether by lack of love from their family and friends or by unjust structures. Many examples of people who remain unfree because there is nobody to actually bring to them the Good News can be shown. There are poor peasants of the northeast of Brazil who do not know how to experience human dignity; there are children (or adults) who believe that they are unlovable and unattractive; there are unemployed who are made to feel like the dregs of society; there are Christians who have been led to believe that God does not love them and who are rejected by the Christian community because they have divorced or have had an abortion. In short, there are all these poor, oppressed and rejected for whom Christ came and who still remain alienated because there is a lack of messengers (apostles) of the Good News. (The urgency of making the Good News real by words and deeds is related to the old concept of the urgency of the Church's mission, and gives a renewed meaning to the old notion of "saving souls.")

A person who brings the Good News to the poor, the oppressed or the abandoned (and it is to them that the message of the Kingdom must come) is not someone who merely tells people that they are loved by God, but rather someone who performs some concrete action, whether it is that of a nurse, or of a revolutionary unionist, or of an individual smiling on the forsaken. Such an action gives content and meaning to the word of the Christian community when it affirms that God loves us. That is why the Church has traditionally felt that its care for the poorest and the critically broken was essential to its mission. The Kingdom is present [3] when, because of what has concretely happened, individuals or groups are able to get up and to say like Zacchaeus: "We are really loved and this love helps us to stand up as persons." Some will add, "In this we have recognized the love of God." Still others will add, "of God who has manifested himself in Jesus." But in any case, it is through this experience of liberation that the Good News is manifested; it is not through a long religious oration. The solicitude of the Church should thus not be so much a transmission of a deposit of faith as a liberating action, even if this action may sometimes be a word.

Such an experience of liberation cannot be purely individualistic. In order to be really liberated, people must feel that they are loved and this will not be possible without deep and collective changes. The theory of liberation, therefore, directs Christians towards social, as well as personal, action. Christian mission is called to blend tenderness, efficiency, analysis and gratuitousness, to be as careful as the snake and as simple as the dove. It asks for a precise and insightful social analysis so that each action may really have the effect desired.

The tension between the proclamation of the total liberation coming from God and its partial realization in actual deeds is important. It is what is usually called the tension between the eschatological aspect of the Church and its concrete reality. Liberation is never realized through some specific action. Consequently no political, spiritual or theological movement can ever claim a complete identification with the Good News. That gift may not be identified with any human representation, even if images are useful and necessary. The Gospel speaks, for example, of a "kingdom" (a political image) or of salvation. For many today, the concept of a global liberation makes sense. But reducing God's gift to any of these cultural images would amount to the sin of idolatry in pretending to possess the total (eschatological) gift of God. Moreover, suffering from a messianistic complex, such a movement would end in being oppressive because anyone who would oppose its ambiguities would be rejected as an opponent of God himself. Unfortunately these "messianistic" movements followed by "spiritual" dictatorships imposing liberation in the name of God have not been rare in the history of the Church, as well as in the history of other religions.

The Church thus is not a group or a political movement which has to gain membership. It is the community of those who found in Christ and his followers the source of their liberation. It is a community whose goal is to celebrate and to effect the liberation offered by God. Thus the Church does not exist for itself, but for the world. It is a place (but not the only place) where the powerful liberation of God is manifested. The Second Vatican Council implied this when it affirmed that the mission of the Church is to be a "light for the nations," and therefore not just a meeting club for believers. Nothing seems less in relation with Christ's call than to establish a church as a "cenacle" where the "chosen ones" could meet and pray. If the Church is not a place where people are concerned to act for the liberation of the oppressed, it is not a sign of the efficient and freeing grace and love of God. But the temptation of a Church related to the middle class culture often is of retreating into privileged circles where salvation is then identified with a "purely spiritual" experience [4] unrelated to societal issues. Such a Church could only witness to a passive God, too passive indeed to face the world with its suffering and oppressions. On the contrary, Christ faced the world. To paraphrase Paul, even if, being of divine condition, he could have remained apart from our alienated world, he chose to be in solidarity with the people, so much so that he finally died, crucified as an outcast. That is how and why the power and the glory of God became manifested in him (Phil. 2:6-11).

DISCUSSION QUESTIONS

1. According to this chapter, what is the good news to be announced?

2. What does it mean to announce the good news?

3. Is the mission of the Church only to transmit a message?

4. How does this understanding of the mission of the Church relate to the bishops' statement according to which "Action in behalf of justice and participation in the transformation of the world are a constitutive part of the proclamation of the gospel"?

5. Are there in the Gospels some grounds for the belief that salvation is a liberation that does not only touch the "soul" but humanity in its wholeness — the whole person and every person?

6. How is the mission of the Church related to the mission of Jesus?

7. Why is it important to work towards the mission of the church? In which sense can it be said that if there is nobody to bring the good news, people will not be saved? Could you apply this to the story of a juvenile delinquent?

8. How can we relate the mission of the Church to the concept of solidarity? Why is it difficult for middle class people to see the mission of the Church as one of a global liberation?

[1]Obviously such liberating action can also be carried out by non-Christians and outside any Christian context.

[2]This obviously implies that "liberation" does not mean simply "doing one's thing," not caring, being irresponsible. Also, since actual society is always partially alienated, there is no complete liberation before the "eschaton", that is, the total advent of God's Kingdom.

[3]As Matthew emphasizes in his tale of the last judgment (Ch. 25), some are not aware of that presence, while they effectively build the Kingdom.

[4]Actually, it is inadequate — and thus, for all practical purposes, false — to identify a spiritual experience with a direct and inner encounter with God. For Christians, the "spiritual" should always be global, thus implicating the body, that is, the physical and the social body.

5
THE COMMUNITY OF THE FAITHFUL

Reflection on the Church is often characterized by positivism and "sacralisation." From a sacral point of view, the Church is considered as a privileged group to which one absolutely must belong, since it is ostensibly the "place" of salvation. Someone living inside the Church is supposed to live in a situation essentially different from that of a person living "outside." This point of view is also positivistic since it presents the Church as a place, a mere object. Moreover, there is an excessive emphasis on materiality in claiming that the Church started with Jesus and then continued in an unbroken hierarchial succession from Jesus until now. Without neglecting the importance of this succession, I want to insist above all that the Church is a community living in "communion," or is a group of persons discovering that they live the same life. We thus do not talk about the Church as a group which one should join; but we shall consider entering the Church as being in communion with a historical community and sharing with it a struggle for justice. But here we are confronted with one of the most serious difficulties of the contemporary Church: not many people feel easily in communion with the institutional Church.

The Church as a Liberating and a Celebrating Community

I shall thus define the Church as a community living the

Gospel and celebrating the presence of Jesus in its midst. These two aspects are extremely important. On one hand, it is a community living the Gospel, living anew, in concrete social, political, cultural, collective and individual acts, the liberation which Jesus has manifested through his Gospel; on the other hand, it is a community which "celebrates" this. Celebrating an event means becoming more conscious of the meaning of one's life through some significant and communal actions or rites. A community living the gospel and celebrating it would of course be a liberating community for society. Such a community does not have as its objective recruiting new members but rather trying to make people and society free by bringing them the Good News of liberation. This, of course, implies as an almost inevitable consequence that some liberated persons will find themselves in communion with this community and will wish to belong to it. These people who have "faith" will ask to enter the Church. Baptism is the celebration of this entry and thus of the whole process of liberation preceding it. By welcoming the newcomer in this way, the community continues and accomplishes the liberation of the one who comes. This introduces us to understand what a sacrament is and what the sacramental structure of the church is.

A sacrament is a way of celebrating what happens within the Church. As a celebration, it refers to a whole life, past and to come, with all its tensions. Moreover, the celebration makes visible and real an always unsuspected possibility, a gift of God. A Christian celebration celebrates the gratuitous gift of God, the struggle of God against the evil of this world (as it was manifested in Jesus' life and passion) and finally the hope of the Kingdom, that is, the society freed and renewed. To understand this process, let us first consider the Eucharist.

The Eucharist as a Sacrament[1]

The difficulty which appears when we consider the eucharist stems from the fact that it has been "thingified" and separated from everyday life. The most typical example is the way in which the theory of "transubstantiation" is frequently understood today. In the framework of a scholastic philosophy of the thirteenth century this theory means that the substance of bread in the eucharist gives place to the substance of the body of Christ. People today do not understand the term "substance" in the same way as it was understood in the thirteenth century. In general, they interpret transubstantiation to mean that what had been bread from the chemical (or any equivalent) point of view before the consecration becomes the body of Christ after the consecration. Now for the philosophers of the thirteenth century, substance did not mean the chemical elements of nature; "substance" referred to the most significant and central element of something. For instance, if I look at my hand, I may say that "substantially" it is a part of myself. Perhaps I would add that accidentally, that is, according to a less significant point of view, it is also an accumulation of proteins. There is, therefore, a distinction between substance and accident, substance designating the deepest aspect of reality and accident whatever else may be observed according to other schemes of interpretation of the same reality.

To affirm transubstantiation signifies that the most central aspect in the eucharistic celebration is the presence of Jesus Christ in bread and wine. There can be no question of conceiving this presence in a scientific or materialist way as one is tempted to do because of the word "substance." Therefore, in the modern world, a word like "transubstantiation" is a very ambiguous term in referring to the eucharist.

Having clarified how the word "transubstantiation" frequently can be misleading, I will now propose another way of seeing the meaning of the eucharist as a whole. It is a celebration in which the Christian community, having throughout a day or week strived to live the Gospel, that is, the liberation of Christ, celebrates this life and the presence of Christ in it.

To do this, it remembers and reenacts the most central moment in the life of Jesus, the moment in which he, who had trusted people, and particularly his friends, realizes that he is finally going to be rejected. With his whole life before his eyes, attending to his Father and trusting his love, he decides that it is better to continue being available and vulnerable to people instead of imposing himself on them through force or violence.

It is then, while with his friends during the last Supper, knowing that he is loved by his Father and because of this, that he comes to the point of giving his life for them. When he says, "Take and eat, since this is my body given for you," he means, "Here is my life given for you." I believe that it is only in this perspective that we may understand what we remember while celebrating the eucharist: we remember Jesus Christ giving his life for us. And he gives his life not because he is being forced by an arbitrary and cruel edict of his Father, but because it is the only concrete way for him to remain available and vulnerable to his friends and to his solidarities. He gives his life in his struggle against the evil present in his society. To be so vulnerable and available in the face of rejection and treason is what Dostoyevesky called the great force of love, a force much more powerful than any other in the world.

In the eucharistic celebration, the Christian community re-lives and remembers this mystery of Christ: he is so loved by the Father and he so participates in God's struggle in history against what crushes people that he gives his life. Therefore, for the Christian community to celebrate the eucharist is tan-tamount to affirming that it wants to live as Jesus did and to declare itself willing to speak as he did: "Here is my life given for you." And this is done in the actual historical situation where people face historical evil in all its dimensions and hope for liberation. To celebrate the eucharist means to place this option of the Gospel in the center of one's life. It means to listen to the "Do this in memory of me," which means first of all, "You too, in memory of me, give your life to those you love." It means discovering the presence of Christ in this Christian community, a presence which is given and which liberates. There is nothing magical about all this. It is simply the expression of what happens in a community centered on the liberating presence of Jesus.[2]

Such a celebration is not simply some kind of ritual apart from what is actually happening in human life. On the contrary, it really changes life. Indeed, to relive in community the gift of Jesus Christ and the actual historical gift of the members of the community, truly it helps to recenter and to be capable of saying with Jesus, "My life, me too — I give it for you." This is why tradition has called the sacraments *efficient signs of the gracious action of God. Signs* insofar as they show that something has happened in the life of Christians; *efficient* or effective since what happens in the community of Christians at the moment they celebrate together is precisely what enables them to live in their own personal and societal history the ever-present gift of God; and finally *the gracious action of God,* or *grace,* since the Christian community also realizes that it is liberated free of charge, not because of all the things it has done, but because it is fundamentally accepted in a justification "through faith and not through works."

In the same way we may consider all the other sacraments. In the limited framework of this chapter, we shall only extend our consideration further to the sacraments of forgiveness and of the sick.

The Sacrament of Forgiveness

In order to understand what the sacrament of penance is, some historical notes are necessary. It is clear that penance as it is known today in the Catholic Church with confession in a dark box does not go back to the origins of the Church. At the beginning, penance existed only for public sins, in particular for apostasy. One of the major questions of the first centuries of the Christian era was, furthermore, to know if one could receive the sacrament of penance several times because penance was the reintegration into the Church of those who had left it. Progressively, however, a new concept appeared in which the role of private penance became more and more important.

This practice was introduced by monks in Ireland and through the missionaries coming from that land, it became very popular throughout Europe. These missionaries wrote "penitentiaries," books which listed, as was the custom in Frankish and Celtic civil laws, the penances to be assigned for each of the sins committed. These recommended penances were conceded such importance that progressively their number became excessive and a deflation took place. The ordinary person could have spent his whole lifetime, plus a few more, trying to accomplish the penances required for his sins. This is why the Church resorted to the equivalent of what governments normally do in such a situation. Governments print more bank notes; the Church produced indulgences. Indulgences originated because, all things considered, it was necessary to find a means to allow people to do penance in a limited time. There was soon an inflation of indulgences, and of serious abuses. It was against these that Luther protested at the time of the Reformation.

But enough for history. Let us try to understand the deeper sense of Christian penance. In a Gospel-like perspective, the life of each person holds a dimension of forgiveness. Each of us has some deficiencies with which we hope to be accepted. In a Christian community it is therefore essential to forgive one another.[3] This mutual pardon is moreover the sign of God's pardon. By a sign of the pardon of God, I do not say that it would indicate extrinsically that God forgives. There is more to it than that. The pardon which people can grant each other is precisely the way in which they can communicate to each other that they are really forgiven, not only at a superficial level but at the deepest possible level. This is one of the most important points of the whole Gospel message: People have the power to forgive sins. This is moreover what the gospel affirms when Christ says: "Sins will be remitted to those to whom you will remit them," or, "What you remit on earth, will be remitted in heaven." These words are not only directed to the apostles but to all people. And the opposition "on earth" and "in heaven" does not refer to two different spheres, but means that what has happened on earth is the ultimate reality of what happens.

In other words, the pardon which we may grant one another is a total pardon. Likewise, and it is important to reflect deeply on it, we can really withhold pardon. This happens when people act in such a way that they block the liberation of a person or a group. The pardon that Christians grant to one another is therefore essential for their liberation. This is the content of the sacrament of penance: the pardon we exchange.

But in order for the pardon to be complete, one has to go beyond the individual dimension so that the Christian knows he is accepted at the Eucharistic table by the Christian community as a whole. This is the role of the absolution granted by the priest, speaker and representative of the Church. For the priest, to grant absolution means to accept in the name of the entire Church, the people of God, the person who comes to the Eucharistic table. To be granted absolution is to know that one is a part of the pardoned people of God who gather around the table.

Absolution is thus the forgiving and real acceptance of someone among and by the people of God. It is thus the efficient sign of the pardon and of the welcome of God. To understand its meaning, it is useful to refer to some liberating experiences as when a priest tells someone, even outside of the formal sacrament of penance: "In the name of the Church, as a priest I declare you are accepted and bid you welcome at the Eucharistic table." Such a word may really bring the liberation of God to those listening to it and make them understand that God forgives them.

Moreover, on the collective level, the sacrament of pardon

proclaims and celebrates the unity of the Church as the assembly of Christian sinners. This unity is indeed not based on an identity of view or of action but on the mutual acceptance of individuals and of groups who, in the name of the same Gospel, sometimes take different options. It is the sacrament of reconciliation which realizes the communion of sometimes hostile brothers. Such seems to be the meaning of the sacrament of God's pardon. But one must admit that the way in which the sacrament of penance is celebrated today seems to be quite inadequate as the present massive neglect of this sacrament testifies. Moreover, much should be said with respect to forgiveness in a more collective dimension. But this would bring us away from the scope of this chapter.

The Sacrament of the Sick

We will bring this brief explanation of the sacraments to an end with just a few words on the sacrament of the sick. I shall not dwell on the way in which it has often been experienced in recent years. Sometimes it almost appears to be a magical and even frightening rite. I want to describe how it could be celebrated in a more positive way. Let us imagine a seriously sick and thus deeply depressed person who has great anxiety and many questions about the future. In the midst of this trial and of the crisis to which it leads, this person suffers and could be very lonely, facing illness and perhaps death.

The sacrament of the sick is the union of the whole Christian community to be with this person in this crisis. Together with the sick one the members of the community will face the trial and celebrate in faith the liberation of God and the hope it gives us. There is, therefore, no need to attempt to get cheap reassurances when confronted with illness or death, but to enter more deeply into the mystery of the gift of God. Such a celebration can really bring liberation to the sick person. It can encourage hope and even give the necessary psychological support for a cure. The community can really be the healing force of God, which comes into action in the sacrament of the sick. That is why the ministry of this sacrament can really be powerful when it helps the community and the dying to face disease, death, separation and hope. That celebration makes sense each time a person feels a deep loss and is thus confronted with death, that is, the complete loss of life.

Reading the Bible

There is no Christian community without some reference to the Bible and its story of God's presence in human history, particularly through Jesus. For Christians, the reading of the Bible cannot be reduced to a search in the Scriptures for the content of our faith. Rather, the Bible is a living word that calls us; it comes from another time and culture, but it still speaks today. And in the written text, Christians find an image of Jesus that can help us to avoid the temptation of creating an image of God that would be too much in our own image. It is not accidental that, in Latin America, a characteristic trait of the basic Christian communities has been the practice of reading the Bible. (In some countries, it goes so far that to be found with a Bible can jeopardize the life of a person identified as a "delegate of the word" because the establishment fears the "subversive" power of reading that helps people to stand up as persons.) Reading the Scriptures and believing in the Spirit brings an awareness that all our liberations are part of a larger movement. They belong to a history of salvation that reveals a powerful Spirit at work in all of human history. The goal of reading the Bible thus is not to legitimate what we already do by claiming — rightly or wrongly — that Jesus did the same. Such an approach would only amount to "co-opting" Jesus and to projecting our own ideas into the Bible. If we read from a broader faith perspective, we find that in the Bible a story much larger than our own is revealed, the story of a God who takes sides in human history and acts for our liberation. The Bible recounts salvation history, the history of God. That history transcends ours, even if we are a part of it and contribute to it. When a Biblical text is read, it confronts and calls people as something *other*; it makes us read our own life with a new perspective coming from elsewhere. (When I say, "coming from elsewhere" I do not mean something external or imposed.) When they read the Bible, some communities discover a breath of fresh air (a spirit) in whom they recognize the Spirit of God. They open themselves to good news that gives hope in the face of their present life.

The reading of the Bible helps Christian communities to construct an image of Christ that goes beyond our projections. The text resists the tendency to reduce the story of Jesus to that of a "purely spiritual leader," or of a "pure activist," or of a "pure healer," etc. — even if it is obvious that every community will emphasize some dimensions of Jesus' story over others because they speak especially to a particular community's condition. Thus, even if the reading of a Biblical text does not take away all risk of remaining enclosed in a restricted religious universe, it can help to overcome the limitations of a too narrow approach.

The Bible does not give any direct answer with respect to the meaning of what we experience today, but it does open us to a dimension of life, to a transcendence. Thus it becomes easier to understand why the Scriptures are looked upon as the place of God's revelation in our human history and as the word which founds Christian communities. Without such a living reading — which implies going beyond individualistic and psychologizing perspectives to a societal dimension — Christianity could easily become just another popular religion reduced to serving as a carrier for a strange mixture of protests of the oppressed and of ideologies legitimating oppression, of varied hopes as well as alienations. It could be that it is not by chance that, in Latin America, a very mixed popular religion has been transformed into faith that is inspiring living communities to take their life into their own hands, just when the people have begun to read the Bible again.[4]

DISCUSSION QUESTIONS

1. What is the relationship of the Church to human liberation?

2. What is the relationship of the Church to celebration?

3. What does the Church celebrate in Christ?

4. What is the relationship of the Church to Eucharist?

5. What is the relationship of the Church to the sacrament of forgiveness?

6. What is the connection between the reading of the scriptures and the Church?

7. Explain what is meant by the statement: "The scriptures always have to be read in a community and with the help of the Spirit?"

---

[1]For a more thorough view of sacraments, cf. G. Fourez: *Sacraments and Passages*, Ave Maria Press, 1983.

[2]The priest's role in the celebration is not a magical one either. As the moderator of the community he is like a "person-sign" of the presence of the risen Christ. Other Christians are also such a sign but each in his or her own way.

[3]Let us emphasize that to forgive or to ask forgiveness does not imply that the person believes he or she is right or wrong. The dynamics of forgiveness are very different from the logic of measuring what is right and wrong. Similarly, mutual forgiveness and God's forgiveness have to be connected.

[4]In that perspective, beyond theology, there is a need for analyzing sociologically the role of the concepts speaking of Transcendence in history. These categories can — in conditions that need to be analyzed — contribute to limit the powers of monarchs and of the powerful. They also can favor commitment in history if they help to create openness to projects that go beyond sheer survival and

cohesion in a group. Some symbols — notwithstanding their ambiguities — can invite a group to be more open to other groups and to the future. For example even if some see the symbol of the priest — supposed to take the place of Christ — as a way to strip the community from its history and to establish clericalism, there is another way to look at this ministry. The priest can — in representing Christ — symbolize for the community the fact that its project cannot be reduced to itself and that it is called to participate in a more universal history. (What is difficult is to enact such a symbolism without too much clericalism!) In the categories of speaking of the Transcendent there can be a richness that a theology too centered on the (very real) immanence of God in history could miss.

6
WHO IS GOD?

Although it may seem strange to talk about God now, I believe it would have been ambiguous to have talked about God earlier. We too quickly presume a set of a priori images or ideas about who God is and about how we can imagine God. But one wonders whether such language has any meaning when talking about God. I mean to suggest that the word God cannot be used as some kind of noun; I don't think it is adequate to say that: "This is God," or "This person is God," as if the concept "God" existed and could be understood. Such an attitude is actually similar to the biblical one which refuses the making of any image or concept of God.

What Is the Meaning of the Word "God?"

Let us draw a comparison. In order to understand what a human being is, it is not adequate to refer to a series of concepts which have to be explained to us from some extrinsic experience. If we want to understand what a person is, we need to meet somebody. For example, through the experience of being loved and loving, a person can truly claim to understand what a *human* relation means. Without referring to an experience of this type, the concept "human" can have a meaning, but this meaning is still extrinsic and superficial. The same is true for the concept of "God": It is only through actual experiences that we can say: "Here I have met God." I believe it is only in this perspective that we can assign full significance to the proposition: "Jesus is God." Such a statement does not imply that we previously had a certain image or a certain concept of God and that we affirm that the person Jesus suits this concept. It is a question of something altogether different. It amounts to saying: "In this experience I am living through something that seems very similar to what many have meant when they claimed that they believe in God. That is why it makes sense for me to affirm that I am in communion with them and to proclaim a presence among us whom we call 'God.' Thus to believe in God does not mean that God "exists" as a human being or as an object exists, but it is to be in communion with those who discovered that, to tell what is the deepest in themselves and in the world, the most adequate (or the least inadequate) language is to speak of a transcendent and loving presence. This could be similar to what the apostle John meant when he wrote: "No one has ever seen God; if we love one another, God lives in us and his love is made perfect within us . . . God is love" (1 John 3:16). John does not introduce us to an abstract knowledge but to the account of an experience related to love and to the encounter of "the one who gave his life."

In meeting this person Jesus, through the stories told in the Gospel, through the whole Christian community and through the eucharist, through forgiveness, through struggles for justice, and through sacramental celebrations, we may go so far as to say that through all this we have discovered God in Jesus. Thus we reach the final affirmation: encountering Jesus has been for us a way of discovering the meaning of the word "God." This is the sense of the Christian proclamation: "Jesus is Lord," "Jesus is God," "Jesus is living among us." When the Christian says, "Jesus is God," he doesn't necessarily pronounce some kind of metaphysical proposition (as the third and the fourth centuries tended to elaborate) through which he would grant the qualification "God" to a man. Rather he refers to the real revelation of God in Jesus. It is not the qualification "God" which explains the subject "Jesus," but it is the person Jesus who makes clearer the meaning of the word "God."

There is no question of an outside God who has to be imagined independently of Jesus and who then would have Jesus sent out of himself to be his revelation. The Christian affirmation means more deeply that, by seeing this person, one has finally seen God. In my opinion this is the meaning of Jesus' answer to Philip who asked him before the Last Supper to show him the Father. Jesus answered, "Have you been with me all this time, Philip, and you still do not know me? To have seen me is to have seen the Father. So how can you say, 'Let us see the Father!'" Actually it is when we see Jesus that we see the Father.

For the Christian the affirmation "Jesus is God" thus is not a proposition explaining who Jesus is, but a proposition indicating who God is. Clearly then it is one of these statements which loses its meaning when one tries a positivist approach. To affirm that we believe in God does not mean we know "objectively" who or what God is but means that we experience communion with the experience of others who also say they are believers. That is also true of the proclamation of the resurrection from the dead. It is not a descriptive statement but a proclamation of hope, which can never be reduced to some limiting specific content. Actually Christian tradition has always recognized that the statement "Jesus is the Lord" is equivalent to the understanding of the meaning of the resurrection.

When people talk about the resurrection, they often perceive it in a reified sacral manner. The focus has been on some kind of a quasi-biological experience of the resurrection of Jesus. In this basically materialistic perspective, one insists heavily on the presence or the non-presence of a body, a corpse, in the tomb and on some material facts rather than on their meaning. The meaning of the event of the resurrection of Jesus is much deeper and has been well explained by Garaudy in his book *L'Alternative.*[1]

The resurrection is not a phenomenon of cellular physiology, a return to mortal life through artificial reanimation. The resurrection is not a historical fact which could be re-enacted with objective witnesses. The place of the resurrection is not in the series of facts and laws of naturalistic or historical positivism. If this were the case, it would have no meaning at all. What meaning would there be in beginning once more a life at the end of which there will be death. The resurrection is not a fact in the positivist sense of the term. Its affirmation of the impossible is a creative act through which history opens the future to all possibilities. It means that our future cannot be stowed away among the series of facts based on the continuation of the data of the past. This appearance of the completely unexpected, based on the continuation of nothing, is the awareness that man is not born to die but to live.

To be a Christian does not mean to believe that the rising from the dead is real (in the sense of history and of positivist science), it means to believe that it is possible. It means not to insert resurrection in the perspective of history, but to perceive history in the perspective of the resurrection. Resurrection thus takes place every day.

To believe in resurrection does not mean to adhere to a dogma; it is an act: the act of participating in the limitless creation, since resurrection is the revelation of this new and radical freedom which the Greek and Roman world ignored. Liberty is no more just the conscience of the necessity, as it was from Heraclitus to the Stoics, but participation in the creating act. This faith is the beginning of liberty.

If I try to decipher the Christian image, to have faith means to perceive that the resurrection and the crucifixion are the same. To affirm the paradoxical presence of God in Jesus crucified, at the bottom of calamity and helplessness, abandoned by God, is to liberate people from the

illusions of power and property. God is no more the emperor
of the Romans nor the man in beauty and force he was for
the Greeks. He (sic) holds no promise of power. He is the
certainty that it is possible to create a qualitatively new
future only when one identifies oneself with those who are
the most destitute and the most crushed in the world, when
one links one's fate to theirs up to the point of not conceiving
a real victory except theirs. This love and the hope for
resurrection are the same.

For believers, thus, the event of Jesus' resurrection trans-
forms the person of Jesus Christ. It is related to the continuation
of Jesus' work by his Spirit, through human works of liberation.
In other words, the Christian experience of resurrection is both
an event and the coming of the Spirit; it is what happened to
the disciples at Emmaus the day of Easter. They were walking
along the road saying that Jesus' adventure had been promis-
ing, but in the end a failure. And then suddenly someone, a
stranger, someone unexpected, joined them and started to explain what happened, using the Scriptures. Interpreting the
Scriptures from a new angle, he showed that it is only through
humble love, through the kind of always vulnerable liberty
which was Jesus', that finally life is born. And suddenly they
recognized Jesus still living among them and thus understood
better who God is.

The positivist definition of the rising from the dead fails to
notice this and leaves aside the unexpected eruption of a life
exceeding hope. This is why hope for resurrection is always
elusive, irreducible to a fact. It is even irreducible to a perspective of survival, considered in the positivist sense of the term.
The news of Christ's resurrection means that the future of
people is open. This is, I also believe, the meaning of this always
mysterious proclamation of the resurrection of each individual.

That is why the discovery of the revelation of Jesus Christ,
with all the unexpected elements and the hope it entails, does
not stop with oneself. It immediately implies a *mission*. The

mission is to bring to others, through acts and in reality, the Good News of liberation, the Good News of the unbelievable gift of God. In this perspective, one understands immediately that the liberation of people depends on persons who either will liberate others or who will not. In this mission, there is no intention of affirming one's own message, to do one's own will, but rather to be the one who liberates, that is, the one who wants to be in solidarity without wanting to impose one's will.

This is what Jesus expressed when he affirmed that he had not come to have his way, but to have the way of the One who has sent him. Christians are also sent to bring the Good News to everybody, not only on the individual but also on the social level. One must in contemporary terms and with modern means act in such a way that "the blind see again, the lame walk, lepers are cleansed, the deaf hear, the dead are raised to life, and the Good News is proclaimed to the poor" (Lk. 7:22). But such a liberation has to happen in a world where people oppress people; that is why it would be unrealistic to speak about liberation and resurrection without speaking also of struggle and of solidarity with all those crushed or exploited by society.

DISCUSSION QUESTIONS

1. What is the main difficulty in trying to explain the meaning of the word "God"?

2. When saying "Jesus is God", does that mean that we know the meaning of the word "God" before knowing who is Jesus?

3. Is the statement "Jesus is God" a descriptive statement?

4. Is the statement "Jesus is risen from the dead" a descriptive statement? Explain its meaning according to Garaudy.

5. Does this section give a renewed meaning to the statement: "Jesus is the revelation of God"?

6. Does the statement "Jesus is God" primarily say something about Jesus, or something about God?

7
STRUGGLE FOR LIBERATION AND CHRISTIAN COMMUNION

Christians do not seem comfortable with expressions like "struggle for liberation." Their reason is quite simple: Jesus Christ has come to invite people to love one another. Why then should we speak positively of a struggle between them? To preach struggle for liberation is felt to be promoting hatred between people and consequently contrary to the communion of love that is at the basis of Christian faith. Because of such arguments, Christians quite often promote political ideologies that conceal the conflicts between people or between social classes or nations.

I believe that such an understanding misrepresents the concept of "struggle for liberation" and that it does not take into account the teachings of the Gospel. In my opinion, struggle for liberation and Christian communion are not contradictory but actually require one another. I do not see how it is possible to live in our contemporary world according to what the Gospel teaches without participating at the same time in the struggle for the liberation of people.

Struggle for Liberation and Oppressing Relationships

It is important to avoid the misunderstanding that might arise by equating the struggle for liberation with hatred between people. Paradoxically, that shift of meaning is frequent among Christians even when they claim to believe in the Gospel that says, "Love your enemies." If that sentence has any meaning, there must be some way to have enemies without hating them. It should thus be possible to fight for liberation without generating hate. Actually, it is only a very individualistic way of conceiving the struggle for liberation which would generate hate. That will be looked at more closely after I have explained the concept.

In view of a better understanding of what we mean by "struggle for liberation," it is useful to consider what is implied when such a struggle is affirmed or denied. To say that there is a struggle for liberation deeply grounded in our society is a way of stating that when our society is carefully analyzed it appears to be built on oppressive relationships. By oppressive relationships we mean relationships through which one party has to submit itself to another if it does not want to lose its security or even its existence. That implies also that these oppressive relationships produce social categories or classes of people who, because of these relationships, have different and opposing interests. That can be the case when we consider blacks and whites, owners of factories and workers, developed countries and third world, and so forth. To speak about a struggle for liberation is then to recognize that people actually are not equal and that this inequality produces oppressive relationships which enslave people. It is not enough to merely recognize social alienation because this does not yet imply recognizing the struggle for liberation. Alienating situations indeed are many and varied. They range from those endured by people living in slums and not knowing why, to business men who are threatened by heart attacks because of the rat-race in which they live. All these people are unhappy. That is obvious. But they are not oppressed in the same way. To speak about oppression and struggle for liberation is to add something, namely, that such an unfortunate situation is not the fruit of bad luck or of fate but rather the result of a social organization in which some people are dominated by others. It is not by chance that people are unhappy: rather unhappiness is the result of oppressive relationships.[1]

On the other hand, denial of the existence of a struggle for liberation will lead one to speak of unhappy people without speaking of oppression and to imply that all these unfortunate situations are the consequence of some fate independent of the relationships between people. It also implies a denial of the specific divergent interests among people. That is why any kind of social analysis which speaks only of unhappiness and not of oppression will never be able to question the reasons for the situation of the poor. Such an analysis thus helps to maintain these oppressive relationships. Consequently, nobody should wonder that dominating groups whose interests are in keeping oppressive relationships as they are, refuse — this is very often a subconscious resistance — to recognize the true nature of some social relationships.

It is well known that for oppressors there are no oppressed. As Hegel and Marx have mentioned, only the oppressed are able to become aware of oppression. To speak then of oppression and of the struggle for liberation simply amounts to refusing to conceal the true nature of social relationships. This does not create division among people, but recognizes it.

Speaking of oppressing relationships can easily be misleading if one pretends that there is within our society a group of people who are solely the oppressors while others are clearly the oppressed. Actually everyone is oppressor and oppressed within the network of relationships in which he lives. Speaking of the alienations resulting from oppression does not mean that only oppressed people are alienated. As Hegel has shown, slaves are oppressed because they have nothing, but masters are alienated because they must defend what they have.

Speaking about oppressing relationships is thus to recognize that the alienations of people come mainly from human relations which are structured in a way that leads people to crush other people. To acknowledge the struggle for liberation is to recognize that when the oppressed become aware of their shared situation of oppression, they will want to free themselves.

A Collective, Not an Individual Struggle

When Christians begin to understand what oppressing relationships are all about, they have to be careful because they have been conditioned for a long time to disregard collective situations and only to focus on individual ethics. They are often tempted to denounce the evil of oppression in a moralizing way. They demand that the oppressors change their hearts so that they can stop oppressing others. Such an attitude is simplistic and inadequate. It is a mistake to believe that all oppressors are individually "guilty" and that their conversion would be a solution. It is not enough to denounce egotistic attitudes. Without denying that there is a certain type of oppression related to individual ethics and that it is to be denounced at that level, Christians must emphasize that oppressive relationships come from social and economic structures that no one can modify alone. Nobody thus is individually guilty even if everybody has a share in a collective alienation.

Christians would probably be able to understand this much better if they would accept the full consequences of the doctrine of original sin which is deeply related to what we are now considering.[2] In both cases, we are talking of a collective alienation coming from the historical condition of humankind. Everyone shares in that alienation and reinforces it by individual behavior. No one has caused it but everyone shares in it simply by virtue of membership in the society of human persons. No one is able to liberate himself or herself from that alienation alone.

The similarity between original sin and the alienation coming from the oppressing relationships is seen in another dimension. As it is only through the mediation of the Christian community (the Church which people enter through baptism) that people will be saved from original sin, so it is only in forming a new human community where the structures of human relations are changed that people are liberated from the alienation resulting from oppressing relationships.

Understanding the structures of human alienation modifies many common ideas of Christians relative to pathological guilt feelings. Feeling guilty because one shares in oppressing relationships is similar to feeling guilty because one shares the consequences of original sin. To feel guilt because of these oppressing structures is often the sign that one keeps a very individualistic point of view according to which a person is concerned to keep personal integrity and to be free from any kind of individual sin. That attitude shares in the same alienation as the very same structures against which it protests. If it is true that every person shares in some egotism and aggressiveness, it helps to realize that these guilt feelings are luxuries. People can only afford them when they are able to maintain a distance from their own situation. That distancing actually means that they are on the side of the dominating groups. At best, these guilt feelings will have some meaning if they help people to go beyond them to fight against alienating structures.

The notion of "hatred of oppressors" reveals the same ambiguity. Many Christians think of it as a personal hatred of the oppressed toward the oppressor. There again, such a personal and individualistic hate would only reproduce the same alienations against which it protests. Actually a less individualistic point of view will consider enemies not as bad persons but as people who, because of the way they are situated in oppressing relationships, are objectively on the side of the oppression. Subjectively they can be good and honorable people. Social analysis that unmasks oppressive relationships does not aim at accusing

these people of personal guilt, but at revealing human alienations and indicating how they can be corrected. This is something many Christians do not easily understand because they
are too attached to an individualistic notion of integrity which
in fact is contrary to the spirit of the Gospel.

It is difficult for Christians who like to be well integrated in
society and who value their individual moral innocence to recognize that, for example, relations between employers and
workers or between teachers and students participate in the
pattern of oppressing relationships. And yet, even if the employer and his employee dress alike and seem almost equal,
one has the power to fire the other; in that respect one is
powerless, the other powerful and in an objectively dominating
position. But when people are in a powerful position, they have
some difficulty in realizing that employers and teachers are
objectively on the side of the powerful and the oppressors, even
when they are subjectively completely dedicated to the welfare
of others. The nature of the relations between employers and
employees, teachers and students, etc. do not flow from their
intentions (which can be very good) but are the objective result
of the economic and the sociological structures of our society.
Obviously a personal hate would have absolutely no meaning
here, and it would not even necessarily help for these "oppressors" to move away from their profession.

But awareness of the nature of relations beween people matters because when it is concealed and when people consider
employers and employees as similar victims of social alienations
of our capitalist society, the difference between them is so denied that any analysis and consequently any liberation becomes
impossible. Such denial actually reinforces the oppressions and
the mutual alienations because it hides their nature. When
there is a relationship in which the employer is objectively in
a dominating position while the employees are in a dominated
one, it would be a mistake to try to ignore or hide the differences
in the name of universal Christian charity. Under the mask of

universal love, the oppressing relations would be concealed and consequently protected. Similar analysis could be done about other relationships, such as racial, the Third World, and even man-woman.

It, therefore, matters to recognize the differences in the relationships between people. Human alienations do not only come by accident or from some fate, but from what can be called a collective sin in which everyone has a part. It would be nonsense to try to determine any individual guilt. That is why it is necessary to speak of a struggle for liberation, the struggle by which the oppressed collectively try to break these oppressing relations and to liberate all people from the alienations these relationships generate.

The Struggle for Liberation and Christian Communion

Is the concept of "struggle for liberation" compatible with the idea of "Christian communion?" Is it possible to reconcile an analysis that coldly and objectively denounces oppressing relations with a "joie de vivre" which seems to be essential to the Christian Good News? We believe that this reconciliation is possible because of two beliefs implied by Christian faith: that a Christian is accepted by God and that it is possible for a Christian community to celebrate the eucharist.

We should first consider that God accepts people as the evangelist John declared so emphatically: "God loved us even when we were sinners." This proclamation is essential since it warns us that, whatever an analysis of the oppressing relationships and of our share in them might reveal, we are basically accepted. Without that acceptance, every analysis that would unmask our participation in these oppressing relations would be almost unbearable, or at least would require such a stoic approach to life that all gentleness and tenderness would be eliminated. Some Marxist movements have not always avoided this. Because of a so-called objective analysis, they have fostered oppressions that proved to be as alienating as those they were striving to eliminate. So while using concepts such as "struggle for liberation," Christians also must be able to celebrate forgiveness in the Christian communion. And that is what the eucharist is all about.

Eucharist, the celebration of the Christian communion, begins with the liturgy of reconciliation. It is essential to the eucharist because it reminds Christians that coming together to celebrate does not mean they are free from all conflicts. They may, indeed, basically be adversaries. It is even possible that there are some dominating or oppressing relations between them and that to be liberated from these, some have to be in conflict with others. It is important to avoid a so-called reconciliation that would be only superficial because it would fail to acknowledge differences and conflicts. Christians who come together to celebrate may very well have different political objectives, be ideologically far from one another, and even be enemies immediately after celebrating together.

The Christian call to forgiveness, however, tells them that something goes beyond their oppositions: that God accepts and loves them. Universal love is not a way of giving a good conscience to one or to the other party. It simply shows that there is something *beyond* the struggle, but that *something* does not suppress or end the struggle. That awareness can save human life from the coldness of conflicts. God's acceptance gives hope to life and enables people to celebrate authentically even when they are aware that justice has not yet come to earth. Even enemies can sometimes celebrate life together. Beyond the conflicts is also the dimension of the feast and of tenderness.

The second part of the celebration, the eucharistic memorial when it recalls how Christ gave his life, invites Christians to live in a mystery which goes beyond everyone. It is the mystery of a Person who struggled, gave himself as a sign of contradiction, and finally accepted being crushed so that others could be free. Such a celebration does not solve the conflicts which confront people, but it gives meaning to the project of those who want to grow out of oppressing relations. Jesus teaches us that oppression will not disappear even if the oppressed are victorious. That would only reproduce oppression in another way. Meaningful liberation comes only in following the One who has given his life freely and faced death. So the eucharist changes the meaning of conflicts between people without suppressing them.

Christians who come together from different classes may well go on being enemies, but not in the same way; they, indeed, have celebrated the way in which Christ endured his own conflicts and struggled to love his enemies. Besides, the communion of brothers and sisters who are sometimes enemies saves the community from the temptation to put off liberation and love to some mythical future. It is not tomorrow but today that people are called to celebrate life through love for one another. Generations need not be sacrificed to some mythical future, whether called heaven or "society without classes"; people are already loved and can love *today*.[3]

Christian tradition, however, has always stressed that there are situations when the eucharist becomes meaningless because the conflicts are such that any common celebration would just be a lie. Furthermore, there are times when celebrating together would be treasonous to the struggle for liberation. For example, what would be the meaning of a eucharistic celebration with Pinochet, the dictator of Chile? There are times when divisions have to be made clear.

Thus such a celebration of the Christian communion does not suppress the struggle for liberation but, on the contrary, recognizes it and reveals its meaning. That is why the eucharist concludes by sending Christians on a mission: liberating people and thus making visible and real the Father's love.

DISCUSSION QUESTIONS

1. In this chapter, is the concept of "struggle for liberation" used as a general interpretative principle for history, or as a means to better explain what the mystery of evil is?

2. What is the difference between alienating situations and oppressive situations?

3. What is implied in the denial of a struggle for liberation?

4. What is the difference between a collective and an individual struggle?

5. Does the concept of original sin help to speak about the struggle for liberation without equating it to a guilt trip?

6. In a situation where there is some struggle for liberation, how is it possible to speak of oppressive relationships, even when the "oppressors" mean well? What is the difference between personal and structural relationships?

7. Is it possible to oppose some people and still to love them and to be in communion with them?

8. How is the Eucharist a sign that struggle never encompasses all life?

9. Are there some situations in which it becomes impossible to share the Eucharist with some individuals or groups?

---

[1]That is why collective conflicts have to be distinguished from individual conflicts. The first ones are related to diverging interest induced by socio-economic organizations. The second are connected to personal antagonisms.

[2]Cf. also: G. Fourez, "Original Sin and Civil Religion" *The New Blackfriars,* July, 1982.

[3]However, complete reconciliation and perfect communion are eschatological concepts. In this life we only have partial reconciliations and communion.

PART 2
Theological Concepts and Existence

8

HOW TO RECOGNIZE A CHRISTIAN CELEBRATION

It is characteristic of communities to band together around specific loyalties and to want to celebrate their lives. Communities that are Christian know that their choices are related to those of Jesus Christ. But the question arises: Do "Christian" celebrations [1] always reflect the choices of Jesus? Is there some way to discern when celebration contradicts the real meaning of Christian faith? Or, to put it otherwise, what does the tradition of the church say regarding Christian celebrations? Does it offer any criteria for discerning the genuineness of a Christian celebration?

The purpose of this chapter is not to describe legislation regarding celebrations or to impose on communities a rigid orthodoxy that would be stifling. A basic premise is to honor the efforts of ordinary people to celebrate the best they can with all their limitations. Moreover, a discernment according to the criteria which will be presented will not be sufficiently meaningful if it focuses too narrowly on one or on a small number of celebrations; such a restricted focus would only highlight the correct awareness that every celebration is limited and can reflect but a few facets of the Gospel and of the celebrating community. A better discernment would encompass the overall pattern of many celebrations by a particular community to verify that community's vision of the Christian mysteries.

It will be maintained, however, that all celebrations are not equal when considered in light of criteria derived from the full tradition of the Church. There are even some celebrations in which it is difficult to recognize the influence of the Gospel.When Jesus made a judgment about the authenticity of the prayer of the publican versus that of the Pharisee, he indicated that not all prayer was equal. With that recognition, we will consider some criteria that theologians can offer when a Christian community wants to discern if what they celebrate is what the Universal Church through the ages has intended to celebrate: salvation in Christ.

In this chapter I will offer four particular criteria for such a discernment. The first refers to the human authenticity of a celebration and can be related to the mystery of the incarnation. It emphasizes that, to be seen as Christian, a celebration has to touch the deepest part of our humanity.[2] The other criteria are specifically theological and are derived from Thomas Aquinas' notions of grace, of the passion of Christ and of the glory of the kingdom as intrinsic elements of the sacraments.[3]

A truly human celebration

A celebration will be truly human only if it touches the deepest core of the event or of the situation it intends to celebrate. This means it should touch — with tenderness — the point of the event that is filled with contradictions, conflicts and even evil — interpersonal as well as collective evil. It is simply false to imply that the world is completely harmonious; such a hypothesis can only be mystifying, obscuring what is really going on and what people are really experiencing. A human celebration begins to be "real" for us when it acknowledges and touches our tensions.[4] To use theological language, the encounter with human contradictions means facing and confessing sin — personal and collective. This criterion places severe judgment on those celebrations that express only harmony in relationships and events. In reality, the history of salvation has always been represented by the image of redemption, an image contrary to the notion of perpetual progress that has haunted our culture from the 18th century Enlightenment onward. Celebrations that conceal or obscure the conflictual dimensions of life cannot be recognized as authentic. If celebrations are to contribute to some change in society, they have to face contradictions and evil.

The seven traditional catholic sacraments provide good examples of the human and tension-ridden content of celebrations. Each sacrament is related to some important human passage in the life cycle from birth to death. The sacraments celebrate the acceptance of a new member in a community which recognizes the oppression or sinfulness that marks society (baptism); recognizing the voice of a new member confronting the community (confirmation); the decisions by which people commit their lives in some way (eucharist); experiencing forgiveness in the face of conflicts (penance); the confrontation with disease or death (anointing of the sick); beginning a family (marriage); the conferring of power in a group (orders). All these events are human situations in which Christians can see the effective and liberating love of God at work.

A specifically Christian celebration

In this section, we will specifically examine the Christian character of a celebration. To call a celebration Christian, it is not enough to speak of Jesus or to pray: "Lord, Lord." Obviously a celebration that never refers to Jesus cannot claim to be Christian, even if a Christian would be able to see evangelical overtones. On the other hand, there can also be celebrations that explicitly refer to Jesus but are based on a value system at odds with what Jesus represents, for example, a celebration promoting some form of oppression such as apartheid or sexism. Such an event cannot be legitimately labeled as Christian, however much it speaks of Jesus Christ.

How does one check the authenticity of a Christian celebration against Jesus Christ and his Gospel? The three criteria offered here will follow the pattern suggested by Thomas Aquinas in his definition of sacraments.

1. The criterion of the gratuitous love of God

We can recognize as Christian a celebration that allows the gratuitous and unconditional love of God to break through, freeing us from evil. To celebrate the gracious love of God (grace) is in many ways in opposition to a moralistic approach. A moralistic approach is concerned to dictate what constitutes a "Christian." A celebration "moralizes" if the emphasis is on "meeting requirements for being a Christian." This is a very different attitude from that of Jesus' God who never measures but gives freely.

For example, I would not recognize as Christian a celebration of the sacrament of confirmation that tries to tell adolescents everything they should do to be "good Christians."

On the contrary, this criterion would be verified in a "confirmation" that celebrates the word of a young person (or of a newcomer in the community) as a gift of God to the community. That word is God's Spirit present in the person to be received. This Spirit can challenge and disturb the community, particularly an older generation, just as the Spirit received by pagans disturbed the customs of Peter and of the first Christians. Thus celebrating confirmation for young people should be a feast acknowledging God's gift of the Spirit among the young, but without denying the Spirit's presence among adults as well. One source of anxiety and conflict in such celebrations is the fear that the young have of their own word. Likewise, adults fear the word of the young. Yet it is within this very tension that communities can recognize a gracious gift: God's Spirit.

In the same way, every sacrament and every non-sacramental Christian celebration is a human ritual which manifests God's gratuitous love freeing that community and the world. I believe that the ritual itself, not some extrinsic factor in relationship to it, is the manifestation of God's love.[5] Thus sacraments truly celebrate the gracious and effective power of God in human history.[6]

This approach has an important consequence: A sacrament is never a celebration involving only one person; it is always a gift for the whole community. The love of God is living and active in the midst of people. In more traditional language, a sacrament is not an individual but an ecclesial act.

2. The "memorial" of Jesus' passion as a criterion

The fundamental story of every Christian celebration is always, in one way or another, God's liberating struggle against evil in the world. This struggle can be seen *today* in the midst of our present historical conflicts, but it can also be seen in Jesus' whole life in which we see him engaged in confrontation. This is especially clear in the case of his passion and death. Similarly, every Christian celebration refers to some initiative on God's part. Our lives must always be situated in relationship with the very struggle of a liberating God. When we get in touch with our own life and struggles, the memory of Christ and of his commitment and confrontations is central to our celebrations. That is why there is a depth of meaning in affirming that our celebrations are instituted by the "struggle of Jesus" which is his passion. That passion can be challenging and energizing in the name of God today. In our celebrations, therefore, we do not only celebrate our own life and struggles, but those of God throughout history.

How then can this criterion of the passion of Christ be applied? This can be easily seen if we consider a celebration welcoming a child into our Christian community. Let us suppose that in the celebration people express how they love the child but never refer to the ambiguities and sinfulness of the actual world in which that infant will grow, for example, to the risk of becoming unemployed, of being sent to fight in a war, or of being indoctrinated by some alienating religious group or political party. Such a celebration can express care for the child, a sense of warm welcome and friendship, but it would not, in my opinion, meet this criterion. It would not help us to get in touch with the contemporary struggle of God against every kind of oppression in our society. On the other hand, when baptism speaks of the ambiguity of the world in which the child is introduced (cf. the concept of original sin), it confronts the community with the passion of Christ. The celebration, thus, will emphasize the hope that in the face of the world's evil, we will not be afraid of naming the evil. (This could be the meaning of using the symbol of "Satan" in baptismal celebrations.) Then the church can become for that child a community that will make visible and real the love of a liberating God in the midst of a sinful world.

I would not recognize as Christian, therefore, a celebration that does not touch the mystery of evil and God's struggle against that evil. In theological terms, it is the same as saying that the Christian mystery is salvation, a redemption or liberation. This mystery cannot be reduced to some notion of human fulfillment or ongoing progress often envisioned in our western culture, especially among the middle class who tend to see life as the pursuit of individual happiness. Christian celebrations are not just any kind of human interval; they originate in the gospels which tell the story of God's struggle in Jesus: his passion. They can never be reduced to a pleasant celebration of our privatized concerns.

3. Hoping for the glory to come: the final criterion

This criterion explains that Christian celebrations mime, anticipate and articulate our deepest longings and hope. They are signs of a new society and a new world: the Kingdom of

God, the new creation. While they express that hope, people also realize they are still on the way to it. In theological terms, this indicates the eschatological dimension of the Christian feast: hope for the reign of God in all its fullness. Thus, we cannot recognize as Christian a celebration that does not express the spirit of hope symbolized in Christ's resurrection.

An efficient celebration of the liberating love of God

When a celebration is lived according to the above mentioned criteria, it has power to change the lives of individuals as well as of groups. People do not come out of the celebration in the same way they went into it; social relationships and feelings are restructured. Believers see in these consequences the very work of God. That is why we say that in sacraments it is really God who is acting. It is one of the places where God is a work, but obviously not the only one. Indeed God acts in many other ways, for instance, through action in behalf of justice. Nevertheless, in Christian celebrations God's action follows the dynamics of a human ritual. Celebrations in accord with the four criteria described here have the effect of the words and deeds of Jesus who enabled people to stand firm, to know peace, and to be whole again. That is how sacraments can be defined as efficient signs that make the freeing love of God — that is, God's grace — break into our society and our lives.

DISCUSSION QUESTIONS

1. In what sense can there be criteria for recognizing a Christian celebration?

2. What is necessary for a celebration to be authentically human? What does this imply for a Christian celebration?

3. What is meant by the statement: "A Christian celebration celebrates the grace of God"? Explain how a celebration could be lacking with respect to that criterion.

4. Do the same for the criterion: "Celebrating the passion of Christ".

5. Do the same for the criterion: "Celebrating the Glory to come".

6. How does a Christian celebration become "efficient"? Explain why a sacrament is not efficient by a kind of magic trick.

7. Explain how the "grace" criterion is related to justification by faith.

8. How do you relate to statements such as "There are conditions to be fulfilled to receive a sacrament meaningfully"? Show how there is a positive meaning to that statement while there is another that would amount to belief in justification by works.

9. How would you handle the dilemma: "Are people committed because of the grace of the sacraments, or are the sacraments meaningful because people are committed?"

---

[1]By "celebration" I mean all the ways by which we get in touch with our individual and collective histories and live them in depth. This is broader than specifically eucharistic celebrations.

[2]When Thomas Aquinas questioned the necessity for sacraments, his answer amounted to saying: "They are necessary because human beings have to celebrate with their whole being the way salvation touches their lives."

[3]The definition of sacraments given by Thomas Aquinas is as follows (*Summa Theologica*, 3a, q. 60, art. 3): "the term sacrament is properly applied to that which is designed to signify our sanctification. In this three factors can be taken into consideration: namely the actual cause of our sanctification, which is the Passion of Christ, the form of our sanctification, which consists in grace and the virtues, and the ultimate end which our sanctification is designed to achieve, which is eternal life. Now as signs the sacraments stand for all of these. Hence as a sign a sacrament has a threefold function. It is at once commemorative of that which has gone before, namely the Passion of Christ,

and demonstrative of that which is brought about in us through the Passion of Christ, namely grace, and prognostic, i.e., a foretelling of future glory." Translated David Bourke, McGraw Hill, NY, 1975.

[4]Even some feasts that appear absolutely joyful take on meaning because of an inherent tension; for example, a harvest feast always refers in some way to the fear that the harvest could have been destroyed.

[5]A concrete example of this would be the unity of body and person: when we see someone's body, we see the person. Thus the body manifests the person.

[6]In reflecting on the efficient change brought about by God's action, the words of Thomas Aquinas in the previously quoted text come to mind: The form of sacraments is said to be in the grace and its *virtues*. These "virtues," if well understood, would not be reduced to the privatized concept we usually have. Rather, they speak of the strength of God at work in the world's history.

9
BAPTISM AND ORIGINAL SIN[1]

When speaking about the doctrine of original sin people often get upset because they have strange ideas about it. For many, original sin is like a curse that is imposed on people from the first day of their life. It is like a spot that stains a little child. Some people reject the idea that a baby, so beautiful and innocent, can be regarded as a sinner. Neither can they understand how a child can be called an enemy of God, and so they want to do away with the whole idea of original sin. And they are probably right in wanting to do away with *their idea* of original sin; but there is another way of looking at this traditional doctrine of the Church.

When we live in any kind of community, we share in all its structures. And merely because we are part of a community, we share some of its alienations. We are deeply affected by them, to the point that our personalities can be modified; our lives are deeply influenced by biological, political, economic and cultural structures. And where a child is concerned, the community in which he/she lives is all the more important because it will form the basic structures of his/her psychology. As modern psychology has shown, our deepest alienations, selfishness and hang-ups arise from our being rooted in wounded families, environments and societies. It is in this vein that we understand what original sin can mean.

Traditionally, original sin is considered something that affects every human being as a member of human society. And

85

through what we have just mentioned, it can be easily understood that, by being part of human society, we share in its alienation. We are in a world where people oppress one another and try to possess things and persons. Being part of such a world touches us even if we do not want it. And when a child is born, these alienations influence the deepest part of the child's psychology.[2] That reality gives meaning to the consideration of an alienation that touches every human being merely because he is a member of the human society.[3]

No one is to be found guilty for that alienation, at least in the sense of a personal guilt; but everyone obviously shares in the resulting situation. Moreover each adult knows that at times he has contributed by his own actions to the reinforcement of these alienating structures. That is also why people are aware that this human situation is not simply the result of chance or of some unfortunate fate; it originates in the history of humankind.

History is obviously made by the oppression of humanity by humanity, and it is impossible for anyone to avoid being involved in its consequences. Thus every human being shares in something that has been traditionally called original sin, which touches each person from the first day of life. There is no individual guilt for that sin, but still it situates every person in a state of alienation because society is alienated. The doctrine of original sin connects the selfish tendencies of human beings with their results in history and society. In our human community, it says no one is clean. That does not mean that a little child is a bad person or an enemy of God, but it is true that, objectively, every child is part of a non-loving community, a community filled with oppression and, therefore, alienated from God. It is true also that, because of the historical situation of humankind, this baby does not have a completely open and free future. The doctrine of original sin speaks about all that, even if it is counter to the ideology which is connected with the free enterprise system and which claims that everything is possible for everyone. It stresses that the history of salvation happens in the face of historical evil in all its forms, individual as well as systematic.

The question then arises: "How is it possible for a person living in a human society to be liberated from basic alienation?" If we have understood the structure of what we call original sin, it becomes clear that there is only one possible way to get out of it and that is to enter into a community of love rather than remaining in a community of oppression. And that is the intended meaning of baptism and of the Church, even if we have to recognize that the reality we often experience in the parishes is different from that ideal.[4] Baptism is like a ritual mime witnessing to a renewed world and society.

Baptism is to be understood as a way of entering a new human society based on the love of God. Obviously, the Church is called to be a community of love, even if it is never completely such a community. On the contrary, it still participates in the alienations of human society and often reinforces them. But, in what it wants to be and in what it is eschatologically called to be, the Church is that community of love which can make people free again. The Church is called to liberate its members by being for them a loving community. That is why there is a celebration in which the Christian community tries to symbolize and to live that tension of people being simultaneously in a community of sin and of love. Baptism, properly celebrated, should be that celebration by which the Christian community affirms itself as a community of love and commits itself to being for the newcomer such a community.

It is obvious that if the Christian community were completely a community of love, it would liberate people from the aliena- tions resulting from the human community of oppression. But as it is not, and as we all share in the community of oppression, the consequences of our historical alienation still touch us. That is what the traditional doctrine tries to express when it says that through baptism, original sin is destroyed but that its

consequences are still present. By what it promises (its eschatological meaning) baptism destroys original sin, but even
when Christians try to share in a loving community they still
participate in an oppressing human society.

The meaning of Baptism, however, becomes clearer as we
see that it is a celebration of the entrance into a renewed human
society which the Church symbolizes. We also realize that the
Baptism of children has a special meaning in as much as it
recalls to the Christian community that it must be a community
of love in order to liberate the newcomer.[5] It is also through
the idea of entering into a community of love, the Church, that
we can understand why traditional theology speaks of baptism
as a sacrament granting faith to the newcomer. To the extent
that the Christian community is liberating and loving, it liberates people and thus communicates the Good News. When
someone entering a community experiences love, the love of
God is revealed to that person. In baptism, this manifestation
of God's love is proclaimed in the name of the risen Christ, an
historical revelation of God's love (and not in the name of any
human institution — always ambiguous — as a family, a social
class, a party, or the Church). Thus Baptism does not give faith
through a kind of magic, but only through the love of a welcoming community witnessing God's love.

When understood in this way, the traditional theology of
original sin and baptism makes sense. It is, indeed, obvious
that everyone needs to be liberated from the alienations of
society; and so there is a need to enter a community of love.
Without that, there is no liberation and no salvation. Baptism
is entering into a community which wants to bring the Good
News; it will thus liberate the newly baptized, at least insofar
as the Church is truly the community of love it is called to be.
That is why the celebration of baptism will only be fruitful
inasmuch as the Church is truly a loving and liberating community, able to be different from the oppressive structure of society.
That is also why it matters that the liturgy of baptism stress

for all the members of the Christian community the place of a commitment to love and to the building of a more just society.

Such a theology of baptism and original sin can seem to be idealistic since no Christian community is truly a community of love, and it would indeed be a mistake to believe that through baptism one will obtain all the benefits from such a loving community. Nevertheless, it is important that the Christian community continue to celebrate the tension in its historical alienation between the Church as conceived by God and by society. That tension will always exist. And the mission of Christians is to build that community of love even though it will always be imperfect. One of the effects of the celebration of baptism, then, should be a new awareness for the whole community of the need to build a loving community to liberate the world from evil.

This theology of baptism and original sin is particularly relevant today as we discover that human alienations come not only from individual actions but from social and collective structures as well. An individualistic interpretation of original sin, reduced to some selfishness in individual hearts, certainly does not take into account the whole theological tradition. The concepts of original sin and of the Church concern not only individuals but also the collective and even cosmic structures of the world. They do not address themselves to individual questions as might be implied by some theological systems. That is why a renewed understanding of baptism and original sin is essential in an era when we become aware of the need to link theological thought and social action.

What we have said about the understanding of baptism and original sin can be helpful to those who prepare a liturgical celebration of baptism. Such a liturgy first has to confront the community with society at large. The celebration should make people aware of the social, economic, sexist, technocratic, political and cultural alienations and of their complicity in these alienations. Then, the eschatological Church, that is, the com-

munity of love as God dreams it, should be symbolized, and
the tension between the community of love and the community
of alienation should be brought to the fore. From that basis,
finally, the entrance of someone into the Church and the commitment of that Church to try to be a community of love take
their meaning. Through such awareness baptism is saved from
an individualistic understanding and recovers its social and
historical dimension.

DISCUSSION QUESTIONS

1. How is original sin presented in this chapter (as well as in
chapter 8)?

2. In the theology of baptism, how does the polarization between original sin and the Church operate?

3. Explain how the statement "Baptism takes away original
sin" has been approached in this chapter.

4. Explain in the same perspective why the consequences of
original sin cannot disappear before the "eschaton" (the comple-
tion of the Kingdom).

5. What is meant by the statement "Baptism is not a celebration of the baptized person, but a celebration of the church"?

6. Comment on the statement: "Baptism gives the faith". Is
the gift of faith a kind of magic?

7. Why is it important that a community celebrating the sacrament of baptism be aware of societal oppression and alienation?
Relate that to the original sin doctrine.

8. Apply the four criteria of chapter 7 to baptism.

[1]For this topic cf. also my book: *Sacraments and Passages*, Ave Maria Press,
1983, chapter 4.

[2]It is worthwhile mentioning that contemporary critics of psychoanalysis emphasize the connection between individual conflicts and the structures of our society.

[3]That alienation can be analyzed through several perspectives, for example, in relation to economic exploitation, or sexist domination, or technocratic programming.

[4]It is obvious that there are communities other than the Church which aim to be loving and liberating communities. God's liberation is obviously not confined to the Roman Catholic Church or to any denomination.

[5]Let us here notice how it is ambiguous to speak of "somebody's" baptism as if only one person were concerned. Actually a sacrament is always the celebration of a Christian community (the Church) even if it concerns a specific person.

10

CIVIL RELIGION AND ORIGINAL SIN [1]

The concept of original sin nowadays is usually not welcomed by most Christians of Western culture. Religious traditions on original sin are felt to be uncomfortably strange in our society[2] where people consider themselves so unconnected to others that the actions of one person are believed to leave other people untouched.[3] Such a cultural agreement is at the roots of a society that believes every person is free and able to achieve whatever he/she wants. Since original sin doctrines clearly deny such "unconnectedness," it is no wonder that they are often rejected and reduced to a teaching as simplistic as a "spot on a child's soul!" This chapter suggests that original sin traditions can speak to our contemporary culture, challenge some of its deepest presuppositions and lead to new levels of awareness of what it means to be Christian in today's world.

To understand the meaning of doctrines which are expressed in what anthropologists call mythical tales or myths, it is relevant to recognize the different representations of the world which grow from different myths, and the effects of those different representations. I submit that a doctrine as "religious" as original sin says a lot about how we envision the civil organization of society. Furthermore, the present disregard for this doctrine is related to social and political myths.[4] I will thus compare

92

the basic assumptions of the original sin myth with another set of assumptions, those underlying the individualistic world view which is summarized in another myth: the civil religion of free enterprise.[5]

Various interpretations of original sin have attempted to articulate individual and collective dimensions of the sinful condition. These interpretations at the same time propose diverse understandings of the relationship between history and our present actions. Classical Catholicism seems to identify original sin with the tendency of each individual toward selfishness and personal aggrandizement. This interpretation is relatively uncritical with respect to the presence of sinful conditions in social and collective historical structures. The main lines of the Reform tradition tend to identify original sin with a kind of complete and irreversible corruption of the structures of the world. Consequently, these structures are often disregarded, and thus accepted unconditionally, while salvation and grace are still regarded as primarily individual and not collective concerns. In this chapter, I will rely on one of the contemporary prevalent interpretations of original sin, submitted by P. Schoonenberg[6] and based on the concept of the "sin of the world". According to this concept, to live is to belong to a community deeply touched by an historical — not metaphysical — sinful condition. This condition not only concerns individual people but also prevailing mentalities and societal structures. It is obvious that, seen from this point of view, original sin will always be either a part of or a challenge to any civil religion.

The "Free Enterprise" Civil Religion in North America

The free enterprise civil religion brings the awareness that many things which had been impossible in Europe became feasible in North America. By so doing, the myth has provided the core of the civil religion of the United States; it contributes to the maintenance of the unity of that society. Free enterprise, however, can also be uncritically used — and *has* been used — to legitimate some of the oppressive structures of capitalist society.[7] Let us examine some of the assumptions which permit the myth to function in this way.

The basic assumption is that all people are equal: for everyone, everything is possible at the moment of birth, and every individual is able to achieve his/her goals in society as it is. This myth assumes that history is something that does not touch the lives of people deeply; hence the social, economic and cultural conditions into which a person is inserted are overlooked. Instead, life is thought of as offering unlimited possibilities, at least if one works hard. Success is attributed to an individual's personal courage and will-power. Each person grows alone, all pulling themselves up by their own bootstraps. The conflicts of life, and especially systemic conflicts of interest, are concealed behind the ideology of tolerance; in the free enterprise mythology, competition is always presumed to be fair.

The "Original Sin" Myth

It is upon presuppositions that are completely contrary to those just mentioned that the most traditional trends of Christian faith base the doctrine of original sin. In this myth, the basic assumption is that history *has* touched persons deeply, to the point that everything is not possible for everyone. By the simple fact of being a member of the human race, people are seen as suffering limitations resulting from past history. Human community is assumed to be a community of sin; in human relationships, people tend to oppress others because of the very way societal life is organized. Thus, persons are born neither equal nor independent of historical conditions. Every individual, simply because he/she shares in the life of society, is limited and partially crippled. These historical limitations are not merely external, but touch each one in the depths of his/her psychology. Furthermore, these injustices and oppressions come from a society that is produced by human choices and decisions and not from an inexorable fate. No one is individually guilty for the fact that there is a community of sin, but everyone shares in this sinful community and is — objectively, if not subjectively — an accomplice to the sin of society. Looked at in this way,[8] original sin has many characteristics of what has been called collective or systemic sin, institutionalized evil, sin of the world, or social sin.

According to the free enterprise myth an individual can be saved alone. In the original sin perspective, however, there is no way of speaking of a merely individual liberation. Outside of a liberating community, one cannot be liberated from the community of sin; salvation is always a societal event. Furthermore, according to the traditional doctrine, no one will be completely liberated before the eschaton, when a true community of love will have replaced the present community of oppression and sin; that hope moves people to work collectively toward their collective liberation.

Thus, contrary to an individualistic way of teaching about original sin, the traditional doctrine relates much more to a collective and even to a cosmic reality rather than to isolated individuals. The fundamental assumption is that, in the very basis of society, there are contradictions and conflicts which, until resolved, prevent anyone from being completely freed.

Free Enterprise and Original Sin as Ideologies

Obviously these two conceptions of society differ greatly and actually are in opposition to each other. No one should wonder, then, that in a society ruled by the free enterprise civil religion, the doctrine of original sin has been seen as absolutely unacceptable. Even more, it has often been reduced to an almost ridiculous theory of a spot on the souls of individuals or to a biological event (a sin transmitted by physical birth).[9] But to those who seriously consider the assumptions of the traditional doctrine or to those who analyze the contradictions of our society, the free enterprise myth becomes unacceptable. The freedom presupposed for everyone in the free enterprise civil religion actually exists only for a minority. It appears as the ideology legitimating those in society who want to believe and make believe that they pull themselves up by their own bootstraps, while actually they are only able to succeed because of their privileges in a non-egalitarian society. "Fair competition," that is, competition between parties on an equal footing is rare and generally not really equal. A good example of false equality would be the relationship between white men and Indians, which was, in fact, the historical basis of the North American free enterprise society. Even now, western society is sustained by a non-egalitarian relationship with developing countries.

The myth of free enterprise and its optimistic conception of society has had all the characteristics of every ideology that stems from dominant groups. These groups always envision society as fundamentally well-organized and free of discord because, after all, they are those who organized it according to their own social position. On the contrary, the myth of original sin, beginning with the assumption that society is basically not well-organized but sinful, seems to originate from the places in society where the poor and oppressed are. From their point of view, society is not well-ordered but looks broken and full of contradictions. For the privileged, the world is harmonious and everything seems possible for every person, but from the standpoint of the oppressed, it is obvious that everyone is touched by the evil of society. Moreover, the human origin of that evil can be verified in the historical oppression to which many people are presently subjected. For the privileged it is as important to pretend that all human beings are equal persons, as it is obvious to the oppressed that some people are more a "person" than others.

The Relevance of the Original Sin Concept Today

The original sin myth is a religious doctrine that, in a very deep way, would involve believers socially and politically. It is one of the ways to express the mystery of evil in terms with which the oppressed can identify. The individualistic reduction which has been prevalent in the recent history of theology is quite intelligible because a culture cannot be based on the myth of free enterprise and at the same time be based on a serious reading of the myth of original sin. It has not been by coincidence that the doctrine of original sin has in recent times been used to demean the value of human beings and to suggest that they should feel guilty and submissive. Such a reading of the myth obviously stems from the ideologies of dominant groups in society. However, when it is not reduced to such an individualistic interpretation, original sin is a subversive doctrine in a society based on the "free enterprise" ideology.[10] Original sin is thus an important concept for those Christians who no longer believe in the ideologies which legitimate, in the name of free enterprise, freedom for the economically, politically and culturally privileged, and oppression for others.

The concept of original sin is thus an instructive example of how the most "religious" doctrines are also social ideologies, or at least functions as such. Actually, it could even be that the concept of original sin is concerned with one of the central social issues concerning religion. Some religions — especially civil religions stemming from the dominant groups — start with a harmonious representation of the world through which its contradictions are concealed. Others accept the challenge of a world historically broken by oppression and exploitation. They approach the world in the hope of its liberation. The traditions of original sin, when taken in their full strength, affirm that Jesus' religion is of the second kind.

DISCUSSION QUESTIONS

1. Why is it so difficult for people in our culture to have a meaningful theology of original sin?

2. What is implied in the original sin myth?

3. What is implied in the free enterprise myth?

4. How do the myths of original sin and of free enterprise oppose each other?

5. What difference does it make to have a world view that includes the concept of original sin or a world view based on the free enterprise myth?

6. How does the original sin doctrine enable us to see humanity as a community?

7. Can you find other religious doctrines that also function as social ideologies?

[1]This chapter has been published in a different form in *The New Blackfriars*, July, 1982.

[2]Many recent biblical and theological studies show how uncomfortable Christians feel with respect to doctrines concerning original sin. For example, Piet Schoonenberg: *Man and Sin*, University of N D Press, 1965; M. Flick and Z. Alexeghi, *Il peccato originale*, Brescia, 1972; A. Vanneste, *Le dogme du péché originel*, Louvain, 1971; U. Bauman, *Erbsünde?* Freiburg, 1970; P. Watte, *Structures philosophiques du péché originel*, Gembloux, 1974; M. Labourette, in *Revue Thomiste* 1970, pp 177-291 and 1973, pp 643-664; Ch. Dugouc, "New Approaches to Original Sin", *Cross Currents*, 28, 2, pp 189-200, 1978.

[3]Cf. M. G. Lawler, "Christian Rituals," an essay in *Sacramental Symbolism*, Horizons 1980, pp 7-36.

[4]A question could be raised: "Does the present disregard for the original sin doctrine originate from its oddity in our culture or from challenging theological studies?" I believe that, from a sociological point of view the answer is clear: theological interest generally results from cultural factors and does not precede it.

[5]The concept of civil religion has been defined in many ways. The following definition by J.A. Coleman in *Theology in the Americas*, Orbis Books, 1976 (Ed. S. Torres and J. Eagleson), seems to be helpful:

"If you like, civil religion is the mystic chord of communal memory always being summoned to reinterpretation in the face of new historic tasks which ties together both a nation's citizenry and the episodes of its history into a meaningful identity by using significant national beliefs, events, persons, places, or documents to serve as symbolic repositories of the special vocational significance of the nation-state in the light of a more ultimate or transcendent bar of judgement, ethical ideals, humanity, world history, being, the universe, or God."

[6]*Op. Cit.,* p 174.

[7]I analyze here the "free enterprise" ideology mainly as it functions now and not as it did when it was the moving legitimation in those who rebelled against the feudal system in Europe.

[8]Such political interpretations of original sin have become familiar to political theologians, e.g., D. Soelle, *Political Theology,* Fortress Press, 1974, pp 86-89.

[9]The concept of transmission of original sin by physical birth has its roots in St. Augustine. However, the Augustinian theology is very far from the popularized theology of the 20th century which tends to *reduce* the transmission to an individualistic biological event. Previously, a biological event was always also viewed as a cosmic and a societal one.

[10]Obviously the same doctrine of original sin would also be subversive for a communist society that would pretend to be perfectly well organized. There is, however, some congeniality between the concepts of "original sin" and of "class struggle." Both notions refer to the belief that before some "eschatological" event (the kingdom or the final revolution), the world will never be free of contradictions and oppression. (And actually both the Church and the Party are sometimes tempted to believe that they are the eschaton.)

11
GRACE

"Grace" is a term in Christian vocabulary which is often misunderstood and used to reflect an inappropriate and inaccurate concept. It is not unusual to hear someone speaking of grace as if it were a small package given to the person by God. Grace is sometimes even seen as a way to accumulate "merits" for the person. In this chapter, we will examine some traditional statements about grace, and we will see that, when they are correctly understood, they are full of meaning.

First, it has always been stressed that persons are saved by grace and not by what they do. That statement has been held uncompromisingly in the Church and arose in opposition to those who claimed that it was through one's own deeds that a person was able to be worthwhile (able to be "saved"). Traditionally, theologies according to which salvation is earned by deeds have been referred to as "pelagianism" and have always been repudiated by the Church.

Second, the Church has always held that grace is a free gift. We need to be reminded of this because of the ambiguities of some popular teaching of religion which present masses, corporal works of mercy, prayers, alms, etc. as ways of gaining grace.

Third, tradition affirms that grace enables people to perform good deeds. And it finally says that these good deeds are effective, in the sense that they truly change human situations. This is the meaning behind the traditional word "merit," a term many rightly question because it leads to believe that "salvation" or "liberation" is earned.

Obviously, these statements can be easily misunderstood. For example, the affirmation that one is "saved by grace" can be interpreted as meaning that whatever people do has no value at all. Actually, many Christians believe that they are not worthwhile, despite the traditional doctrine of grace which states that we are worthy, because of the gracious love of God. Another misconception has arisen from the statement that one cannot do anything to obtain grace, and that grace is a pure gift: some understand this as if they should not do anything, and as if every human commitment was worthless.

Because of the ambiguous meaning of the doctrine concerning "merit," it is easy to see how often people tried to accumulate "merits," making the Christian life a kind of competitive race where each one attempted to gain the prize. But there is another way to understand what the doctrine of grace is all about. In view of that, I will suggest two keys to understand that notion. The first one is to understand the word "grace" to mean "the gracious love of God." The second suggestion is to use the experience of being loved as a key experience to enable people to understand what the theology of grace means.

Let us investigate some elements of the experience of being loved in order to grasp its similarity with the doctrine of grace. When I discover that I am loved and if my experience is deep enough, I do not claim that I am loved because of some personal qualities. What I say finally amounts to: "It is amazing that he or she loves me and that love has changed my life. The love of that person has reached me. It gives another meaning to the world, and to my life in that world. It frees me and liberates me. It is not by myself that I am saved or liberated but through that gracious love." Then the person proceeds to say, "There is nothing I did which makes me deserve that love; it is completely gracious. I wonder why I am so loved? I did not do anything to gain or to deserve it." Then going on, I would probably say that "Love has changed my life to the point that I now realize how I can relate to others in a new way. I see how that love gives me wings so that I can act in a way I would never have dreamed possible." Finally, I could add that "Love has so transformed me that I can behave so that people's lives around me change; I can also love others and truly do something meaningful in this world."

The doctrine of grace says almost the same thing. It speaks of the liberation and the change brought to people by the gracious love of God. It stresses that the most important part of Christian faith is not *doing something* even if that something means loving others. Christian faith is the experience of first being loved, of being liberated and saved by the love of God made visible through the love of people. That is what the doctrine of grace is all about.

People are saved or liberated by the gracious love of God, and that love is carried to them through the love of people. They are not saved by what they do, by their deeds, but they are saved by that gracious love which reaches people without having to do anything to gain it and with no strings attached. That is the meaning of the statement "people are saved only by grace."

The assertion that one cannot do anything to obtain grace has an obvious meaning in this context. Love is something which touches people in a completely gratuitous way. Such an experience changes their lives. That is why the gracious love of God has been called "efficacious grace." To people who realize they are loved, God's love gives them new wings; they can fly anywhere! They can do many things they would never have attempted before. Thus grace is truly efficient. And that change is not only for individuals, it is also intended for the collectivity of people.

God's gracious love changes people so deeply that they become able to love others. That is the underlying meaning of the doctrine of merit. One can then see why a conception of merit which makes it a kind of bargaining power is wrong. Similarly, it is obvious that grace is not a magic package which people receive, a "thing" God gives them. The doctrine of merit means that what people do when liberated by the gracious love of God can liberate others; people are changed and become able to discover their worth. The "worth" of persons is actually created in part by the love of others.

Thus, when it is said that grace "gives merit" the understanding is that the gracious love of God eventually changes the lives of people in a way that enables them to be different and worthwhile. This statement is emphasized in opposition to those who say that the gracious love of God resulted only in an external or superficial liberation without enabling people to be really free and lovable by themselves.

On the contrary, the doctrine of merit stresses that the gracious love of God is powerful enough to help people discover that they have a new power by which they finally are able to help effect the liberation for themselves and others through their own deeds. That is how theology joins here a theme traditionally acknowledged by psychologists: people want to be recognized for their own sake. The Catholic doctrine on grace emphasizes that we are loved both gratuitously and for ourselves.

God's gratuitous love — grace — can remain a very abstract or even an empty concept unless it is made visible by people's concrete actions. Actually, the usual path of Christians does not begin by acknowledging to be loved by God. Rather, it is when people discover that they are accepted — either through interpersonal or societal experiences — that people are able to find meaning in the statement: "God loves us".

And this summarizes what the theology of grace is all about: It is not because people do something that they are loved by God or by people, but because they are loved by God and by others, they can, through this love, perform good deeds which

liberate people at the individual, as well as at the collective
level.

DISCUSSION QUESTIONS

1. How would you express the concept of grace in plain, meaningful English language?

2. What positive meaning can be given to the theory of "merit"?

3. Explain the statement: "We are saved by grace".

4. What is the relationship between the "justification" theology
(see chapter 2) and the concept of grace?

5. How can we give a meaning to the statement: "We have to
make visible the invisible grace of God"?

6. Can there be a socio-political dimension to the concept of
"grace"? in which sense?

12

SACRAMENT OF FORGIVENESS

Traditionally forgiveness has been an important aspect of Christian faith. The message of Jesus is obviously connected with the remission of debts and with how persons forgive one another. Part of his Good News is forgiveness of sins. That is why the sacrament of forgiveness is very important to the life of Christians. They will be freed through the forgiveness of people, which is a sign of the forgiveness of God.

To understand the place of forgiveness, it is good to remember how alienating social structures are and how these alienations touch everyone. Consequently, it is *de facto* impossible to live that Christians hold to the practice of confessing sins to one another and of requesting forgiveness.
we want to ask for that person's forgiveness. This request for forgiveness obviously does not stem from an unhealthy sense of unworthiness. It stems from the experience of the limitations of our love.

It is striking how people can have deep loving relationships despite the fact that they are limited and may hurt one another. But the awareness of limitations, even though painful, does not cause despair when people know that they are loved. It is, in fact, amazing to realize that one is accepted graciously, even without deserving it. That does not produce a masochistic self-denial. On the contrary, the awareness of one's limitations and shortcomings becomes a thrilling experience when it is accompanied by the feeling of unconditional acceptance. That feeling does not imply that an accepted person will not try to overcome his limitations; but the paradox of being loved just as we are reveals to us the graciousness of love. That is how the Christian should always be thrilled by the "amazing" grace of God who never measures.

Unfortunately, this awareness of a need for forgiveness has often been transformed into an unhealthy, moralistic approach. While the sacrament of forgiveness should be the celebration of that amazing love of God and people, it has often been transformed into a trial. It is not rare that people who approach the sacrament of forgiveness feel that they must be judged by an exacting God. Thus, instead of a joyful celebration of forgiving love, the sacrament becomes the *awful* experience of submitting oneself to scrutiny. The practice of the sacrament of penance in the Catholic Church has become so meaningless that many Christians have given it up. Unfortunately, there is a danger that while giving up that practice they also lose the possibility of a meaningful celebration of forgiveness which would foster the awareness that mutual forgiveness is a sign of God's forgiveness.

How then could Christian forgiveness be celebrated? Traditionally the celebration begins with an avowal of sins. Confession of sins becomes meaningless when people begin to count their mistakes and shortcomings in order to have something to say. But it makes much more sense when people request forgiveness in a healthy way. To understand the meaning of such a request, let us first recall how we feel when we find ourselves isolated from another and do not dare to reach out.

The feeling can be illustrated in a situation which does not involve the need for forgiveness but does show the difference made when one person requests something of another. For example, as a guest I may be reluctant to request a glass of beer. As long as I dare not ask, I remain isolated. However, when I feel able to ask for the beer, my isolation is broken. To request something from someone is a deep experience; it is the beginning of trust. We know we trust someone when we can ask anything, knowing we will not be rejected even if the request is not granted. Thus, the experience of requesting is crucial in human relationships. It is even more so when forgiveness is requested.

To ask for forgiveness is to trust, knowing full well one's shortcomings. It is like presenting oneself naked before another. To be able to do that is a liberating experience. To ask for forgiveness is also to get out of the logic of the scapegoat, a logic by which it is always the "other" who is guilty of the suffering in this world. When it is understood from that angle, confession of sins and the request for forgiveness reveal their meaning. To go to others and to ask them to accept us, as we are, without masking our deficiencies, is really the beginning of a deeper relationship.[1] When we hurt another, we experience a painful bond between us; asking for forgiveness makes this hurt a basis for a true love. Consequently, it matters very much that Christians hold to the practice of confessing sins to one another and of requesting forgiveness.

It is only through the experience of confessing to one another in a caring relationship that the meaning of the term "sin" becomes clear. Sin, in this perspective, is not the transgression of an abstract moral law; it is not even defined by the concepts of good and evil; sin is not a confrontation with ideas, but with persons; it is defined in a relational way through relationships. We request forgiveness "for sins" and we can face the ultimate meaning of sin only when we feel accepted and loved. That is why Pascal said that we can realize what our sins are only when they are forgiven. So asking forgiveness of one another is not only a healthy practice but it is essential to the growth of deep relationships. As long as two people do not realize that they have hurt each other, and as long as they do not ask forgiveness, their relationship remains superficial. They have not yet deeply touched one another's lives. Thus, the request for forgiveness is an essential part of our relationships with one another and with God. When done in this spirit, the request for forgiveness can help people to be transformed from "guilty persons" into "sinners," that is, people able to live forgiveness. To give a name to the sin and to confess it is an important part of the process of forgiveness. That can go much beyond interpersonal relationships. As the Bible makes clear in many instances, it is also meaningful to name collective sins or systemic sins in which we all participate, would they be racism, sexism, exploitation, imperialism, and so forth.

"May we forgive one another?" is a very important question for human beings. It is important because our shortcomings and mistakes can leave us helpless if we do not forgive one another. In many cultures, people believe that when they have transgressed taboos or have offended someone, forgiveness is not available. In opposition to that, the teaching of Jesus is clear; people can forgive one another and he invites them to do so. He invites people to forgive again and again, whatever the sins may be. And when people do, the unconditional love of God is manifested. Jesus affirms that the forgiveness that people grant one another is the forgiveness God grants to them once and for all: "Whatever you have forgiven will be forgiven in heaven."

The way, then, that we forgive one another is the way the love of God is manifested to people who, then, know they are not justified by works, but by the gracious love of God. Consequently, the celebration of Christian forgiveness should never be a painful event, but it should produce healing and joy as it frees us of the burden of having to be perfect in order to be acceptable. Obviously, that acceptance is not an invitation to continue hurting one another. We know, on the contrary, that people who are aware that they are graciously accepted want to act according to that realization. They do not want to hurt one another but to love much because they feel they are forgiven much.

What we have said sheds light on the practice of the sacrament of forgiveness. It should not be looked upon so much as receiving forgiveness because God accepts us, but as a celebration in which people become aware that they are forgiven because they are accepted. It should by no means be a frightening or painful experience, but it should be a true celebration of one of the most human dimensions of life. Christians should then remember that they are called to bring to one another the message and the reality of forgiveness. Jesus, led by the spirit of God, dared to forgive sins. Christians in their turn are called to do the same in memory of Jesus.

The forgiveness of sins obviously is not reserved to special ministers. Every human being is called to forgive others. When people do so, the forgiving love of God is manifested. And when people refuse to forgive us, it is difficult for us to experience God's unconditional acceptance. It is a deep responsibility for human beings to realize that, through their refusal to forgive, they can prevent the unconditional love of God from being manifested.

We now want to address ourselves to the question of the ministry of the sacrament of forgiveness. When Christians forgive one another they certainly are ministers of the forgiving love of God. Is there then a special role reserved to special ministers, such as priests? In the Catholic tradition, it is emphasized that only the priest, recognized and ordained as such by the Church, can give absolution. That is often understood as a restriction on the power of people to forgive one another. But if we are aware of what absolution means, we see that the particular role of the priest does not limit the power and the calling of other Christians.

When the priest gives absolution, that human person acts with an official mandate from the Christian community to welcome a person to the eucharistic table. To give absolution is thus to accept a person as a full member of the Christian community, the people of God. From that point of view it is obvious that only a recognized and commissioned minister can speak in the name of the complete community. The absolution of the priest thus stresses the communal dimension of the manifestation of the love of God. When a priest, as the official representative of the complete Christian community, the Church, gives absolution people are enabled to realize that they are not only accepted by individuals but by the entire Church. Absolution completes the celebration of the sacrament by making known that the forgiving love of God is present and should be present in the whole community.

But it is obvious that the sacrament would not be fruitful if the absolution were not connected with a true mutual forgiveness.[2] Thus there is in the sacrament a tension between the eschatological dimension (that is, the Christian community called to be the complete manifestation of the forgiving love of God) and the reality of the present Church, still very imperfect and repressive. A total fruitful celebration of the sacrament of forgiveness would need a Church, and a society, completely freed from all alienations. The celebration of the sacrament is a sign of the total gift of God, which is not yet realized completely. That is why forgiveness should not be confused with reconciliation. People or groups can live forgiveness and still be enemies and go on fighting. For example, there can be meaningful forgiveness with respect to racism or sexism only on the condition that the struggle against racism or sexism goes on. Similarly, forgiveness with a marriage does not necessarily mean that the problem at stake is settled.

DISCUSSION QUESTIONS

1. Why is forgiveness a necessary dimension of meaningful human relationships?

2. What is the difference between asking for forgiveness and

"having a guilt trip"?

3. How is the experience of sin related to that of being forgiven?

4. What does it mean to be transformed from "guilty persons" into "sinners"?

5. Explain how human forgiveness is necessary so that we can find a meaning in divine forgiveness.

6. In the sacrament of forgiveness, how does human forgiveness signify God's forgiveness?

7. How is it possible for human beings to "retain" sins?

8. Relate the absolution by a priest to the communal dimension of the church.

9. Is it possible to forgive without being yet reconciled? (for this question, cf also chapter 20).

---

[1]Asking for forgiveness, however, does not necessarily mean that we believe we were wrong. The dynamics of forgiveness is deeper than the rationality of rights and wrongs.

[2]Another question would be the investigation of the relationship of the sacrament of forgiveness with societal conflicts. How can Christian forgiveness be lived in a class conflict, a race conflict, etc.

13
PRIESTHOOD

It is easy not to understand the meaning of charism and the sacrament of leadership in the Christian community because the priesthood has been so often connected with unfortunate abuses of power in the ministry. According to Jesus, no one in the community should be called Father or Rabbi or Master because all are brothers and sisters. Besides, the leaders in the community, if they desire to follow Jesus, should be as servants. To understand what a meaningful priesthood is, it is important to reconcile what the Gospel says about the brotherhood of Christians and the service of leaders in the community.

Let us first consider what a Christian community is. It is a group of people gathered by Jesus Christ and his followers through the Good News. They are together because Jesus has in some way touched all of them. Therefore, it is correct to say it is Jesus and only Jesus who gathers the community. No other member of the community does this. That is reflected in the traditional teaching of the Church: that only Jesus is a priest. That means that he alone gathers the community and leads it to his Father. When Jesus leads the community, it is in the name of the Father, not in his own name as if he were taking power for himself, since he does not want to impose his leadership of priesthood or his will on the members of the community.

Because we can no longer see Jesus Christ as his disciples did, his priestly ministry is taken over in some way by the community itself. It is the community as a collective group gathered in his name who exercises the liberating ministry of Christ. Through the community Christians minister to one another. It is only through the members of the community that the liberation of Christ can come to us. That is why, second only to the priesthood of Christ, there is the priesthood of the people of God, of every Christian. Each Christian is called to exercise this priesthood as Jesus did — to liberate people, to gather a community celebrating and living the eucharist, and to forgive sins. Thus, the ministry of the priesthood is first exercised by Jesus Christ and then by every member of the community.

Because the Christian community is a human community, it will have structures, and the way power is exercised in the community should be subject to evaluation. In a Christian community, as in any other group, there will be some who will exercise more leadership than others. The ministerial priesthood stems from that social structure. Some, for example, will be better than others in helping to liberate people and in carrying out the forgiveness of Christ. These people are charismatic leaders.

The relationship between these charismatic leaders and the institutions of the community is an important question. Those with charisma of leadership can be in a difficult situation if it is not clear that their charisma is related to the good news in Christ and that the community accepts and recognizes leadership. If it does not, they would impose on the group and, finally, they would be its oppressors. That is why official recognition of charisms is valuable to a community. If someone's charisma of leadership is recognized and if the Christian community (the Church) commissions that person to exercise leadership, then the community will protect itself from the undue dictatorship. On the contrary, if one attributes the leadership of the Christian community to oneself (the ministerial priesthood), one might destroy that community by enslaving it; one could also promote a personal and inappropriate interpretation of the Good News. None of us, therefore, should take over the priestly leadership without a commission from the community. That is the purpose of ordination; the sacrament of orders recognizes the tensions involved in conferring power and at the same time makes clear that power in the community does not belong to anyone; it is received as a gift from God.

The ordination to the priesthood should be the celebration by which the Christian community recognizes and receives the charisma of leadership as a gift from God. It should be the recognition in a person of a charisma given by God; it bestows on that person the mission of leading the community. Despite all the tensions related to power, that leadership, which is intended for the liberation of the people, is not perceived as something the community provides for itself but as the gift of liberation received from God. Thus, through the sacrament of ordination, the Church at the same time constitutes itself and receives itself as a community.

This is a theologically sound way to proceed with ordination.[1] When a person shows some charisma of leadership, he or she would be ordained to serve in that community[2] and thus become a person-sign of Christ's presence. The charisma of leadership and its recognition by the Church should be the basis of a vocation. People should not be ordained because they received seminary training, but because they are good leaders for the community. Ordination can be called a sacrament because it is the celebration of a gift of God and because it makes effective that gift in the community.

Obviously, the leadership of the Christian community (the priesthood) should not function in the same way as it does in a society where leaders are oppressors, lording it over the people. That is what Christ meant when he stressed that leaders in his community should not be like the princes of this world. But such a temptation is present in the Church, and everybody knows that the hierarchical Churches sometimes yield to that temptation.

The question of the validity of ministries is important to some Christians; therefore, it can be useful to learn more about it. It is not an easy thing to deal with because the concept of validity has often been badly understood and confused with the concept of fruitfulness or reality of a sacrament. A sacrament is said to be valid when it is officially recognized by the whole Christian community (the Church) as a sacrament, a communal and effective sign of God's liberation and love among us. A sacrament is real or fruitful if it is celebrated in such circumstances that it liberates people. The two concepts are thus different. Some celebration could, for example, be not valid but still fruitful. That means that it would not be recognized officially by the Church but still be a true epiphany of God in his community. On the other hand, a celebration could be officially recognized but absolutely void of any true liberation coming from God. That becomes obvious when we consider the example of marriage. Some marriages can be valid, that is, recognized according to all the rules of the Church and yet not be fruitful or real because of a complete absence of love. On the contrary, some marriage celebrations could be invalid because some rules for official recognition have not been fulfilled, and still be a true epiphany of the gracious love of God.

The concepts, thus, of validity and reality have to be carefully distinguished. And as validity is related to some official recognition, even in case of conflict, we can only speak of validity in juridical terms. Juridical rules, indeed, are tools to solve conflicts of official recognition. If, for example, the memorial of the Last Supper is celebrated by a group without an ordained priest, it is obvious that, according to the rules of the Catholic Church, it will never be officially recognized. But it could well be that such a eucharistic celebration would be much more real, fruitful, and full of the presence of God than some "valid" celebration.

If no one in the community doubts the validity of some sacraments or of some ministries, it can be useless to consider that concept; it only has meaning when there are conflicts. Obviously, if that does not cause any problem, Christians will try to have valid sacraments and ministries. But if it would present serious inconveniences, some theologians believe that it could be appropriate not to worry too much about validity. The concept of validity has been obviously overemphasized, sometimes at the expense of the concept of fruitfulness. It may, indeed, happen that stress on validity can destroy the Christian community, leading it to neglect more important values like charity, justice, or for example in the case of the priesthood, the liberation of women. However, the official doctrine of the Church emphasizes that a sacrament will not be valid unless presided over by the appropriate minister.

Enough on the validity of the priesthood. The fact that a priest has been officially given a mission for the community to bring the Good News to people should be emphasized. In accomplishing that mission, it is important that the priest fulfill to the end the mandate given and dare to take personal responsibility to be like Jesus: above the rules, the laws, and the traditions of the ancients, so that people can thereby become more free. A ministerial priest is not just a professional, acting as such where his services are requested and then forgetting the person with whom he had a professional relationship. The ministry of the priesthood encompasses the person as a whole. It is through these existential actions of people that God's action is visible. The priest's personal relationships with the Christian community are not then superficial, but deeply mark his life. That is probably what the now out dated theology of the priestly character tried to convey.

People have not been ordained to the priesthood just to apply regulations or rules but to help the Christian community to become truly free and liberating for the world. If ordination is exercised in that spirit, the ministerial priesthood will reflect adequately and make visible Christ's own priesthood.

DISCUSSION QUESTIONS

1. What did Jesus say about those who would be leading communities? What is the problem with calling priests "fathers"?

2. Describe the relationships between the priesthood of Christ, the priesthood of the people of God, and the ministerial priesthood.

3. Relate the charism of leadership and the priestly ordination.

4. Is validity the only concept by which a celebration can be evaluated?

5. Analyze some differences between what it means to be a priest and what it means to be in other positions of leadership or in helping professions such as psychology or social work.

6. In which sense can it be said that a priest (like every Christian, but in a different way) is called to speak "with authority"?

[1]Most often Catholics speak of priestly ordination, but there are other ordinations, or commissions, in the church. The Christian community organizes its ministeries in function of the particularities of each situation.

[2]Unfortunately, it is often the contrary which happens; instead of looking for people exhibiting the charisma of leadership and ordaining them, people are often ordained for other reasons. This is probably one of the causes of the crisis of the clergy.

14
MINISTRIES AND CHURCH STRUCTURES[1]

For some years now, changes have been taking place in the way the organization of the Church is viewed. There are many signs that the bishops and clergy recognize that their role and their position are increasingly questioned. While appearances remain much the same, something really is changing. The significance of these modifications depends on a person's position in relation to the Church. For believers, these changes may affect their perception of their Church. For some non-believers and believers, these changes are also interesting symptoms by which they can evaluate the lines along which our culture is evolving, especially concerning questions of authority. The following pages will describe how some theologians interpret these events. Special reference will be made to the monumental work of Bernard Cooke, *Ministry to Word and Sacraments* (Philadelphia, Fortress Press, 1976). This lengthy study (some 700 pages — the numbers in brackets refer to pages of this book) discusses how ministries have evolved with the Church, and puts forward theological conclusions that radically challenge ideas currently held on priesthood, episcopacy, and organization of the Church. It follows the line of the many studies on ministry made under the impact of the Council over a ten-year period, which have cast new light on several aspects of this question. Bernard Cooke's volume on ministry, as well as a recent study by Edward Schillebeeckx,[2] provides from a particular perspective, a comprehensive presentation of recent findings in the controversial area of the theology of ministries.

The Bases of the Theological Development at Vatican II

The Vatican Council laid the foundations of a whole theological reflection on the subject of the Church and ministries. It is well known that the Roman commissions which prepared the document of the Church had structured it in a pyramidal fashion: first, Jesus Christ, then the Pope, the bishops and the clergy, and finally the people of God. Underlying this, a very hierarchical conception of ministries could be seen: Jesus as the supreme priest, the Pope as his vicar on earth, and then the bishops, the clergy, etc. When the Council met, the bishops rejected this conception and replaced it by another. Jesus, mediator and priest, is the direct foundation and head of the Church, the people of God. The priesthood of Jesus should be immediately followed by the priesthood of the people of God, a global entity and sacrament of salvation. Only then comes the ministerial priesthood: the Pope, the bishops and the priests. This implies an important change in comparison with the first conception. In the document approved by the Council, ministerial priesthood is seen in the perspective of the collective priesthood of the whole people of God; in the first design, the participation of God's people in the priesthood is indirect, through the clergy. The details of this change may be argued, but the concrete effect is clear; it is a total change in perspective as to the way of situating the Church and the hierarchy.

This new view had its impact at two levels. On the one hand, concretely speaking, a number of church practices have changed and some of the abuses of clericalism have been suppressed; at the same time, it is clear that authoritarian resistance and reflexes have curbed this evolution. On the other hand, on the basis of the Council document, numerous theological reflections were made. American bishops, faced with a profound crisis of the clergy within their dioceses, commissioned a study some ten years ago which was to be psychological, sociological and theological. For several reasons — some of which are not hard to guess — this study was not much appreciated or used.

Within the framework of these investigations, Bernard Cooke, then a Jesuit and director of the department of theology at the Jesuit Marquette University, Wisconsin, started a lengthy work on the historical and theological evaluation of Christian ministries. This is the book he has now published as professor of Religious Studies in Windsor University, Ontario. The work clearly indicates the present direction of theological reflection, after the historical studies set in motion by the Council. Accordingly it may be expected that some of its results will have an increasing influence on concepts of the Church and of ecclesial ministries in the years to come.

The issue

For Cooke, the central problem is undoubtedly the fact that "the notion of 'priesthood' that prevailed in Roman Catholic circles for many centuries was formed in a period of history when legal categories were the dominant way of thinking about human society, whether ecclesiastical or civil" (20). The way ecclesiastical roles were understood was influenced by concepts related to civil functions. Other important influences were the theology of the papacy, parish structures, clericalism, and, in addition, the fact that everything done by the clergy was increasingly attributed to the power conferred by ordination — an apparently logical shift, but unfounded theologically. The author also refers to the deficient instruction given in seminaries, especially concerning the notions such as "sacrifice," "sanctification" and "consecration." To find a way out of this blind alley, Cooke proposes for consideration the notion of Christian community: "perhaps in deepening the notion of 'community', studying the particular way in which Christianity is meant to be community, and examining the non-structural elements of Christian community, we can discover the ways in which certain persons (or groups of persons) can function in ordered fashion to foster that community" (24).

When he considers what a community is, Cooke wonders about the models which have been used to represent that community. When represented as a moral entity (our holy mother the Church), it runs the danger of becoming so external that "the bulk of Christians have lost for many centuries the sense of themselves being the Church; 'the Church' is this other reality to which they are related through faith and religious practice" (194). The models which were used are numerous and varied: cosmological (an element of a mythico-cosmic geography), military (crusade, fortress), monastic (withdrawal from the world). But most important would be the political model — the celestial city — which would eventually determine the representation one has of the nature of authority in the Church.

With this model in mind, the author raises one fundamental question, central to the whole of his thinking. "It may well be that the course of action open to us is not a shift from one political model (monarchy) to another (democracy) but entirely away from a political model" (192).

More fundamentally still, he suggests simply letting the Christian community be what it is without trying to make it fit into other categories. The view he then develops is very simple; all reasoning that tries to define authority and ministries in the Church by using political models should be abandoned, so that one can come face to face with the unique liberating and sacramental dynamic of the people of God, in whom the Spirit and the risen Christ dwell. This orientation opens totally new and indeed revolutionary perspectives by refusing to rubber-stamp the take-over of the Church by any particular model. At the same time, it forces the Christian community to acknowledge the workings of the Spirit in its midst, making possible the institution of new ministries. Cooke points out also that the institution of ministries by Jesus can be understood as continuing through the presence of the risen Christ in the church.

The Historical Development of Ministry or Ministries

Before developing the way in which ministries are understood, we must first of all, through historical analysis, grasp how the significance of certain elements has become restricted. We can thus discern, throughout Christian history, a tendency to limit to the ordained clergy the role of actively representing Christ. People seem to have forgotten that tradition and apostolic succession were at first a function of the whole Church (196) and not simply a ministry specific to the episcopate, although the latter is "one of the special ministries that exist to sustain and nurture the corporate ministry of the Church" (203).

One of Cooke's contributions is the notion of the Church's "collective ministry"; for him, certain ministries (services) are carried out by individuals, others by "collectivities" or groups, while still others are functions of the whole ecclesial collectivity. In that sense, tradition, apostolic succession, and the magisterium are part of the collective ministry of the Church and are accordingly not attributed to individuals only, nor even to "colleges" such as the bishops.

The conclusion of the author's analysis is that within the Church there is no place for "rulers"; there are specialized ministries, but they do not have a superior status or the status of ruler. He insists on the fact that there does not seem to be any ground for attaching special efficacious power to any charge. He suggests that "the 'objective power' attached to the activity of those ordained for sacramental ministry derives from performing an action as a sign of the Church's faith. Because some persons through ordination possess public recognition as witnesses to the Church's faith they are enabled to act as a 'word' of the Church; but the effectiveness of their actions comes from that action being the Church's word and not from some other power that is attached to the office which a particular person occupies" (199).

One of the basic questions raised by historical study is whether there exists a fundamental charism (the episcopate) of which all other charisms (prophecy, teaching, healing, etc.) would be elements or whether we should speak instead of a diversity of charisms and ministries.

The history of Christian ministries seems to be clear: the pastoral charge tended to absorb the other ministries and this gave birth to the present pyramidal structure of the Church. But can it be concluded with certainty that this de facto absorption is essential de jure? Cooke wonders whether, at the beginning, the episcopacy was the central collectivity with which the presbyterate was associated (the situation we know today), or whether the presbyterate was the basic collectivity in which the bishop had a specific role.

Historical evidence seems to support the representation according to which the Church was first run by a college of elders among whom the bishops had a special governing role. In the course of history, the presbyterate (assembly of elders), as known by the early Church, disappeared but it had functioned through a collective leadership rather than ministers of worship like our present-day priests. As the episcopate become more and more important, the "elders" (presbyters) became, in the service of the bishops, like deacons with somewhat greater powers although they often preferred to consider themselves bishops with reduced powers.

Cooke's theological conclusion is that it is, finally, preferable to talk about specialized ministries (in the plural) rather than about a global function or a single charism called "Christian ministry."

The diversity of ministries should not be limited once and for all; the norm of their institution would merely be the need of the Church at a given moment. Bernard Cooke sees such an ecclesial institution in continuity with the tradition of the institution of ministries by Christ, because "if one accepts the belief that the Church is truly the body of Christ and animated by his Spirit, then the risen Christ himself and his Spirit remain involved in the developing historical life of the Christian community, and no element of the creative unfolding of the Church's being can be seen as purely human and not 'instituted by Christ'" (204).

The Detail of the Ministries

As to detailing the ministries in the Church, Cooke starts by indicating that "leadership is not a specific function, much less an office" (208) and that "the attempt to absorb all the various ministries into the episcopal function seems unjustifiable" (203). For him, "the basic ministry is not that of governing (episcopein) but that of prophecy" (209). But this ministry cannot be institutionalized and, consequently, cannot be the object of an ordination.

He then mentions other ministries such as teachers (didaskaloi), a title that was carefully avoided by priests in the primitive Church, apostles (itinerant ministries), and theologians. Speaking of liturgies, he stresses the tradition of faith according to which "God 'uses' the ministers of sacraments to sanctify the people" (210). As far as the episcopate is concerned, Cooke sees a general evolution towards increasingly greater "supervision" and less direct ministerial activity. He points out that the concept of "pastoral charge" is ambiguous, as it seems to presuppose a way of governing the Church distinct from the ministry of the Word and the sacraments: "It is the word of God that must govern the Christian community." In this perspective, it makes no sense to suppose there is a pastoral charge to govern the community quite distinct from the service of the Word. Besides, such a charge would be derived from "political" models of the Church.

This theological reflection recalls the discussions of theologians about the famous medieval distinction between "jurisdiction" and "order"; it suggests the theological way to break away from a church which, in the name of jurisdiction (government of the Church) became increasingly clerical by basing its organization on the structures of the civil, juridical society.

As for the role of the celebrant in the liturgical service, Cooke sees him, on the basis of history and theological reflection, assuming two principal functions. The celebrant symbolizes the collectivity of ordained ministers, and thus establishes a link with the Universal Church. Furthermore, as a sacrament within a sacrament (that is, himself a sign in the midst of a significant ritual), his function is to help, in the very act of the collective liturgical celebration, a living liturgical community to exist (336). The author refers, in this context, to the fact that during a whole period in the history of the Church the sacrament of Orders did not designate, as today, the ritual of ordination, but directly the body, the college, of priests. In that sense, it is the ministers themselves who are considered to be sacraments, visible signs of the love of God uniting his community.

The Bishops and the Magisterium

In regard to bishops, the author raises a number of questions on their role in relation to the Word. He does not view them as teachers as such, but thinks that "the collegial witness of the Twelve was substantively normative for primitive Christianity's faith, and that this normative function continues in the episcopacy and, as far as we can see, must continue in some such collegial witness. What does not seem to be necessary is that the group performing this special ministry of collegial witness be the group in charge of governing the social existence of the community" (338). This leads Cooke to deal with the question of the "magisterium."

His opinion is differentiated and clear. "In the light of historical and theological reflection, there seems no justification for appropriating 'magisterium' to one group or one ministerial function, even that of teaching. Instead, 'magisterium' is the interaction of various kinds of teaching (prophecy, preaching, teaching, liturgical celebration, etc.), each of them normative in a somewhat different fashion. The entire Christian community shares in this magisterium, by the Church's corporate reality as sacrament, and by individual members exercising one or more teaching functions. Thus, the classic division of members of the Church into *docens* and *discens* (teachers and taught) needs to be revised; in various and complementary ways all members of the Church are both *docens* and *discens*. The witness of the episcopal college teaches the entire community, but so also does the experience of Christians living their faith in family and business and social involvement. The technical clarifications of theology must be listened to by bishop and factory laborer, but the theologian must learn from the eucharistic liturgy that he celebrates along with bishop and factory worker. Everyone in the Church must learn from all the others and must help form the faith of all the others" (339).

Conclusions

It is impossible to summarize in a few pages all the results of a historical and theological study of such scope which discusses the numerous theological studies published in the last decade and puts them into the context of history.

The main thesis of the work is clear; by insisting that the ministries are at the service of a Christian community, itself a sacrament of God's love, and that they do not stand above the Christian community, the orientation of this work is in line with that of the Second Vatican Council.

By not presenting a democratic model of the Church to replace a monarchical one, the book breaks with a long ecclesiastical tradition that considers the Church a political society. Thus it meets the demands of the theologians who insist that the Church should not be assimilated with political groups. But, by the same token, by breaking down the clerical model the book opens up a fundamentally eschatological perspective that is not without connections with the utopia of self-government, a community where ministries would be a function of its needs. At the center of this vision, the word of God is active in the living Church.

Masterly though this work may be, it seems to have its limitations. I will mention three of them. First of all, out of an undoubted desire to free theological reflection from a lack of "scientific" depth in some episcopal positions, the author repeatedly stresses the importance of theological method: "intellectual comprehension and scope have their own authority." He also stresses academic methods and the confrontations they presuppose. One might, however, wonder if, in taking this line, the author may not be running the risk, in the name of science, of giving special status to methods that are relative and, after all, somewhat arbitrary.

More fundamentally, one of the limitations of the work seems to be the construction of an ecclesiology that appears, in theological terms, to ignore the doctrine of original sin. In sociological terms, it neglects the factor of domination. I think, in the end, that the history of ministries in the Church can only be understood against the background of a society in conflict in which relationships of domination prevail. In other words, I think it is necessary to construct a theology that takes into account the fact that any "office" in a community tends, society being what it is, to become a way of dominating. After all, the most explicit words of the Gospel concerning those who "lead" the Christian community, address precisely this point: "that they shall not be like the princes of this world." This opposition seems to me to be a possible basis for a theology of ministries. By rejecting all political models, Bernard Cooke makes a step in that direction. It may be possible to go even further and to show that a theology of ministries can only be achieved in opposition to the ideologies that legitimize various kinds of oppression in our societies. Such a theology could integrate elements of economic, political, and ideological analysis. It would no longer be ahistorical, but a function of the mission of the Church: manifesting the love of God in a society that is concretely and specifically marked by sin. In the line of the liberation theologies, it might produce, I think, a theology of ministries that is more dynamic than the one proposed by Cooke. Finally, one other limitation. Many readers will regret that the author has paid so little attention to the place of women in the ministry.

But let us stress once again the massive character of the work he has done by clearing the field. This work will undoubtedly give rise to many lengthy discussions. Some may reject its conclusions, while others believe that it opens up the way to fruitful discussion. But it is obvious that the questions it raises and the orientation it suggests will mark the theological thought for years to come.

DISCUSSION QUESTIONS

1. How did Vatican II change the Catholic perspective on the Church?

2. What does Cooke mean when he says that the notion of priesthood has been influenced by civil categories?

3. What does he mean when he says that the model for the church should not shift from one political model to another?

4. What does Cooke think of a so-called global charism named "Christian ministry"?

5. How do most historians of the church view the socio-historical development that led to the pyramidal model of the church?

6. What does Cooke mean when he speaks of the priest as a sacrament within a sacrament? What role does he see for the priest in the liturgical celebration?

7. How does Cooke see the Church performing its mission of witnessing to the Word and teaching about it?

[1] This chapter is an adaptation of an article published in *Communiautes et Liturgie,* Jan. 1978, pp 17-24, translated into English by *Pro Mundi Vita,* Oct. 1979.

[2] Edward Schillebecckx, Ministry: *Leadership in the Community of Jesus Christ,* New York, Crossroads Books, 1981.

PART III
Existential Concepts and Theology

15
THEOLOGIES AND IDEOLOGIES

When Christians seek to proclaim the Good News, they try to explain what they mean by saying that God offers liberation. And so they begin to elaborate theologies. A theological system is a conscious or unconscious way of speaking about the Christian message and of making it relevant to some situation. Consequently, any kind of theological thought expresses what human life and human society is. A traditional way of saying this is that every theology presupposes some philosophy. A theological system thus is not only an expression of the Good News, but it is an interpretation from the point of view of a given group and situation. That is why any kind of theological thought can be said to be an ideology, a system of thought explaining from a specific historical situation what life is all about.

When we speak about ideology we are using the term in a broad sense which includes any type of legitimation for an individual or a group. It is obvious that each time we express how we see the world that we do it from a particular point of view. That is why there are not absolute but only relative ideologies and why each ideology reflects the situation of those who produce it. It expresses their beliefs, experience, and involvements. When dominating people speak about the world, they see it from their position of domination and they produce ideologies quite different from those who are dominated.

So when we consider an ideological system it is relevant to ask whose interest that ideology defends. Moreover, there is a need for some analysis to unveil the relationships between an ideology and the interest of those who construct it. An ideology must be judged, not only by the intentions of those professing it, but by its objective effects on society. For example, an ideology will be named oppressive if it maintains oppression, notwithstanding people's intentions.

What has been said about ideologies is also true about theologies. Theological thought not only stems from the gospel but also from the social, economic and political situations of theologians. A theologian working with government people will probably think quite differently from one invoved in the inner city. So each theology has to be analyzed to make obvious its political point of view. Actually theologians who are politically aware will analyze that themselves. Many theologians, unconsciously perhaps, maintain the ideologies dominant around them. When this is so, their theologies have, without their even noticing it, the ideologies of the dominant groups of society. Every theology can be analyzed from a political point of view by the question: "Whose interests does this ideology represent and what are the objective effects of this theology on society?"

Some concrete examples can demonstrate this phenomenon. If, for example, a theology insists on the concept of obedience, the social function of that emphasis should be recognized. That was illustrated by the novel, *Uncle Tom's Cabin*. The novel reveals that some religious ideologies on obedience have the political function to keep the poor submissive. That example also demonstrates that what is supposed to be a purely "religious teaching" actually has many important social and political functions. Almost every kind of theological statement can likewise be analyzed. It is enlightening that some theological formulations flourish when they represent the interests of the dominant group, while other theological ideas decline when they oppose the dominant ideology. For example, the doctrine of original sin is intolerable in a society based on the ideology

of free enterprise because it indicates that there is some alienation and lack of freedom touching everybody. That is a scandal
for a society based on the myth that every individual is absolutely free. To be confronted with a theology that states each
individual is alienated by the structures of human society is
threatening — too threatening. That is why the dominant ideology will oppose such a theological doctrine and finally reduce
it to the innocuous and even silly concept of a kind of hereditary
stain without any true social meaning.

Original sin is an interesting example because it shows that
an apparently "purely religious statement" is actually also a
powerful ideology. To hold the doctrine of original sin ultimately
means to denounce the presuppositions of the free enterprise
mythology which claim we are in a world where everything is
possible for any individual. Thus the theology of original sin is
deeply political and has important implications for the way
Christians will react politically.

Another interesting example of the ideological conflict underlying religious thought is the difference between a theology
which stresses healing and reconciliation and another which
emphasizes liberation. The former envisions society as a natural or biological process and does not acknowledge the fact that
if there are no oppressive structures in society, the need for
healing and reconciliation would practically disappear.[1]

A theology of liberation, on the other hand, denounces these
social oppressions. A theology of healing will be acceptable to
dominant groups, but a theology of liberation threatens the
interests of the dominant groups in society; consequently it is
not so easily accepted. It is remarkable how a theology of healing
or reconciliation can serve as an effective tool for oppressors
by the way it conceals social conflicts. Thus one can understand
how theologians are politically involved in these ideologies,
even when they do not know it. Even the most basic and apparently apolitical statements have to be analyzed from a critical
point of view.

For example, when Christians say that it is important to care for the individual, there is, besides an expression of care, an underlying ideology which focuses on individuals rather than on the people as a whole. Oppressors can use such an ideology to prevent any kind of collective change. Stressing that the care and the concern for the individual can be ideologically ambiguous is not to say, however, that persons should not care for the individual. Rather it is to emphasize the possible impact of that theological ideology. The "concern for the individual" ideology supports private property, free enterprise and the rights of those who already have power: it is often an excuse not to change the structures in society. That example is obviously not an academic one, since the rich in Europe used Christian individualistic doctrines, prevalent during the nineteenth century, to defend themselves against the just claims of the working class. And, as it often happens, Christians were not aware of the ideological content of their theology.

If Christian faith is always expressed in theological doctrines which are also ideologies, it is obvious that religion cannot be separated from its political impact in society. Some theologies have been used to defend the interests of oppressive groups; others are and will still be used for that purpose. On the contrary, some theologies can also be a powerful ideological tool for the liberation of the oppressed. Obviously only the second kind of theologies can bring the Good News to people. It is thus important to have ideologically liberating theologies.

A concern for theologies congruent with the liberating news of Jesus has appeared recently, especially in South America and in western Europe. In South America it has been called the theology of liberation. This term means a theology which proclaims the Good News and, at the same time, is ideologically a tool for the liberation of the oppressed. In Europe, this kind of theology has been called political theology, that is, theologies which have integrated in themselves all the tools of political analysis.

Such theologies do not try to reduce theology to politics but to articulate the message of Jesus within the present situation of society. Thus they accept that, from a political view, they can be considered as ideologies among others, and they believe that they have to take into account the actual effect of their statements. Moreover, these theologies recognize that the contemplation of Jesus' life is generally subversive in a society organized according to alienating structures. It is only when that impact of theology is taken into account that theological thought can begin to be part of the announcement of the Good News. Moreover, if the Good News is to liberate people, the objective ideological effects of the theological doctrines are not only side effects. Rather, the liberating aspect of the theology is an intrinsic part of its worth.

Christians, however, have often been accused, and not without reason, of supporting oppression; we should, therefore, be particularly careful about the ideologies carried by our theologies. What is probably the most dangerous pitfall for us is an "idealist ideology," that is, a moralizing ideology which does not really analyze the concrete and economic roots of alienation. Even some so-called liberation theologies fall into that pattern when they are more interested in denouncing abstract injustices than in transforming actual economic and political structures of the world. People are not liberated because ideologies are unmasked but because structures of society are so transformed that people can have power. Liberation must happen not only at the level of ideological superstructures, but also at the political and economic level.

When speaking of political theology, one should be careful not to think of it simply as a search for theological legitimations for political actions. These can be useful, and it is obvious that the Scriptures can be inspirational for socially committed people. But, aside from broad inspiration, the Gospel will never indicate exactly what liberating actions could be meaningful today. Looking at the political and economic oppression of people today, and remembering Jesus, Christians will have to find for themselves relevant policies and strategies. The Gospel will never legitimize either nonviolence or revolution, but some people, inspired by the Gospel, can decide for such strategies because they are led by their analysis of the situation and their vision of the future of humanity. However, it is true as Johannes Metz emphasizes in his "political" theology that the memory of Christ's life can lead Christians toward subversive and re- volutionary actions in our present society. Christian faith should not be confused with a political vision, but Christians should recognize that, in a definite political action, their hope and their faith begin to be put into practice. The attitude that prevents confusing any particular political action with Kingdom is what has been called the "eschatological reservation" which saves us from both idolatry and fanaticism. It also cautions us against the danger (not always avoided by Christians) of ab- solutizing our own plans and of being unable to be happy with the human condition, however limited it may be.

DISCUSSION QUESTIONS

1. How is the term ideology used in this chapter?

2. How do theologies become ideologies?

3. Explain how, in the case of the doctrine of original sin, theol- ogy and ideology interfere.

4. What is the aim of so-called "political theology"?

5. What is the meaning of the concept of "eschatological reser- vation"?

---

[1]It is interesting to see how social ideologies speaking of "healing society," or "curing its disease" portray society as a passive "patient" plagued with some ill for which nobody is responsible. Thus these ideologies will suggest using techniques able to cure the patient while hiding the underlying social and political conflicts. Theologies of liberation, on the contrary, will not speak with these *natural categories* but will rather use political concepts.

16
IDEOLOGICAL ANALYSIS OF RELIGIOUS TEXTS

When a group of people pray together, some in the group may feel very much at ease with the content and style of the prayer; it fits the way they experience God, life, and themselves. For others, the reverse may be true; the communal prayer is at odds with their experience. This phenomenon indicates that religion always conveys an image of the world, or in other words, an ideological content. To analyze various ideological forms that stem from religious expressions and the way in which they are conditioned, I will distinguish three levels of conditioning. The first level is related to a given civilization, that is, to all the socio-economic and cultural structures of a society; for instance, a feudal society, the Roman Empire, our industrial society, or the Mayan civilization. The second level of conditioning refers to the diversity of social categories or classes. For example, in a feudal society, aristocrats did not have the same type of religious expressions as the peasants. Beyond the traits that are common to all who were part of the feudal culture, some elements were specific to each social class. And finally, the third level recognizes that individuals of the same social or even family origin can have different life histories. These specifically individual histories also condition each person's psychology and, finally, religious expressions.

Thus a kind of religion much impregnated with guilt feelings can be related to a civilization as a whole, or to a particular social class, or to personal circumstances. For example, as Mary Douglas suggested, guilt may characterize a society surrounded by enemies. Or the poorest in a society can often be conditioned to feel guilty, and their religions will reflect that fact. Or finally such guilt can be related to a specifically personal evolution, e.g., because of having had parents who were too authoritarian.[1]

In this section, I will consider only the variety of religious expressions related to social classes. For that purpose, I will use a very simple — almost simplistic — analytic framework to distinguish three social classes: the ruling class, the middle class and the oppressed. I will analyze several religious texts which show a variety of "religions" drawn according to class lines. My goal is to help the reader to realize that our communal religious discourses — like the prayers we use to speak to God individually — do not just fall from heaven, but are rather specific socio-cultural productions which reveal how closely religious and ideological discourses interact.

The Religion of the Ruling Class

By ruling classes, I mean these social classes that truly have decision making power with respect to polities, for example, chief executive officers of major corporations. In nineteenth century Europe, the ruling class included the high bourgeoisie and a part of the aristocracy. What is typical of this social class is an awareness that they rule society and have some real power in it. Its members know very well that they are involved in societal conflicts but they are not afraid of this involvement; they even seem to enjoy the challenge and they are ready to assume the necessary risks. However, since they are usually protected from the worst consequences of social tensions, they tend to have some difficulty in getting in touch with the suffering that afflicts those who do not have their privileges. When people have only to nod to get what they want, it is very difficult for them to perceive the hopelessness of those who are at the bottom of society.

In our consideration of texts produced by ruling classes,[2] let us look first at the Canticle of David in the second book of Samuel, chapter 22: *"The Lord is my rock, my fortress, my deliverer. . . . my shield, the horn of my salvation. . . . Praised be the Lord, I exclaim, and I am safe from my enemies. . . . With your aid I run against an armed band, and by the help of my God I leap over a wall. . . . I pursued my enemies and destroyed them, nor did I turn again till I made an end of them. I smote them and they did not rise; they fell beneath my feet. . . . My enemies you put to flight before me and those who hate me I destroyed. They cried for help, but no one saved them . . . trampled them down. . . . You rescued me from the strife of my people; you made me head over nations. A people I had not known became my slaves; as soon as they heard me, they obeyed. . . ."* In such a text, David faces his responsibility as a chief of the people. He is not afraid of taking sides, and of deciding who are his allies and who are his enemies. He lives with these conflicts. But he does not seem to have much sympathy for the suffering of his enemies and these he destroys. In the background of this canticle, one senses the unceasing temptation of ruling classes to use God and religion to legitimate their power. Such a use of religion was evident in the motto inscribed on the belts of Nazi soldiers: "Gott mit uns" (God is with us). The same tendency is manifest in the reply Cardinal Spellman made to a reporter who questioned him as he was blessing the troops in Viet Nam: "Right or wrong, it is my country."

Teilhard de Chardin's writings offer a second text written from a ruling class perspective. *"Yes, I hope that the Lord will use us as much as possible, you and me, for the great task of making manifest to today's world today's Christ . . . a focus of energies that create and energize the world — where there is suffering indeed — but mainly a fire, the only fire able to have the universe progress, now that it has become conscious."* What seems to me to be typical of a ruling class mentality in this text is Teilhard's awareness of world concerns. Instead of dwelling at length on interpersonal relationships, he immediately focuses on the global progress of the Universe. Such a perspective — typical of the ruling class — can be very inspirational. But the feeling of being a part of the birth of a new world can often prevent the members of the ruling class from perceiving individuals and their lives. It is probably not by chance that Teilhard — a medic in the French army during World War I — wrote, right in the middle of a cruel battle, a poem on the world that was to emerge from the kind of butchery which that war was. What he, as an aristocrat, sees is that a new society is being born; but he seems somewhat blind to the suffering of the soldiers killed or maimed in the process and the suffering of their families. Quite often ruling classes perceive what is not going well, that is, what is evil, but they do not seem able to truly analyze it as such. For them, evil is usually quickly integrated into their "reason" (often "reasons of state") and their concept of efficiency. To emphasize that Jesus' death was an execution may appear to them as a scandal, and they will tend to prefer crucifixes where Christ is shown as a king rather than as a tortured marginal person.

For the ruling classes, religion may function in one of two diametrically opposed ways. When religion is perverted, those in power use God for their socio-political objectives. A religion which legitimizes their power serves to dull their sensitivities to the point that they no longer see suffering around them — especially when they themselves are responsible. However, religion can also serve to challenge those who have power. Traditionally, religious discourses — at least when they retain some authenticity — confront princes by reminding them of some limit to their power, for example, by emphasizing that they will be judged by God. Moreover, Jesus' death, that is so easily erased in the religion of the powerful, can become another call. If, indeed, God has chosen to suffer as a human person and to be executed as an outcast, should we not have a better look at the suffering of our fellow humans?

Finally, if, as Christians, we want to confront the religion of the ruling class with the Gospel, we may recall a saying of the Gospel: "How difficult it is for a rich person to enter the kingdom;" but Jesus also added, "For a human being, it is impossible, but for God, everything is possible."

The Religion of the Oppressed

The oppressed share with the ruling class a deep awareness of societal conflicts. They know — even if it is often difficult for them to articulate it — that they are the little ones who are always crushed, and that conflict is for them a way of life. For them, liberation seems real only when it touches every aspect of their life; a merely "spiritual liberation" does not make sense for them. For any liberation to be real for them, there must be economic, political, and cultural components. The poor know that they have to struggle to get somewhere. But, unlike the ruling class, they know very well the price to be paid — their own suffering, the suffering of the poor.

Their religion, with the religions of every social class, is filled with ambiguities. On the one hand, many poor look at themselves — that is, they have been conditioned to look at themselves — as if their situation is a natural one. Their oppression is reinforced by a religion which has them internalize an image of themselves as inferior people who must be submissive to those who have power. Such a religion can rightly be called an opiate of the people. In reference to such a religious approach, sociologists often point to discourses emphasizing obedience to bishops, popes, princes, parents, managers, and every kind of superior. On the other hand, there are also many religious texts that express the aspirations of the oppressed classes when they want to stand on their own feet. These texts are sometimes produced by the people at the grassroots, but they are more often written by intellectuals who are in solidarity with the poor. When they truly listen to the oppressed, these intellectuals can express the latter's feeling and write in such a way that

the poor become concerned. The following pages will analyze
some of these religious productions.

A Christmas Carol

In French speaking countries there is a very popular Christmas song called "Minuit Critiens" (It is Midnight, Cristians").
It was written in France in 1847, one year before the popular
revolution of 1848. At that time, ideas were fermenting among
Europe's poor as Marx wrote his famous "Manifesto," while, in
France, a leftist magazine was published with the title, "The
Republican Christ" (in contrast with Christ the King worship-
ped by the well-to-do who were monarchists). The song became
very popular but most of the upper class absolutely disliked it.
Even in English translation, the words can explain why:

*"It is midnight, Christians, it is the solemn hour when the
God-Man came down to us, to erase original sin, and stop the
anger of his Father. The whole world is thrilled with hope in
this night that gives it a savior. People who are kneeling, wait
for your liberation. Noël, here is the redeemer." "The burning
light of our faith led us to the cradle of the child, as in the past
a sparkling star guided the rulers coming from the East. The
King of Kings is born in a humble crib; powerful ones of the
day, bold with your grandeur, God speaks to your pride from
there. Bend your head before the Reedemer."*

*"The Redeemer has broken all the bonds; the earth is free and
heaven open. He sees a brother where there only was a slave.
Love unites those who were together in chains. Who will tell
him how grateful we are? It is for us that he is born, suffers,
and dies."*

*"People standing up, sing your liberation. Noël, let us sing the
Redeemer."*

To analyze this text, let us first notice the strong awareness
of distance. Here, the universe is not presented as a basically
fair and pleasant world where everybody enjoys equality and

partnership with everyone else. The text speaks of the "God-Man who came *down* to us." And the next sentence can even be more startling to our contemporary middle-class mentalities. We do not like this image of an angry father. However, when we go beyond personalistic and individualistic representations of original sin and when we consider the societal disorder and oppression that the concept unveils, the sentence becomes meaningful. It expresses rather well the situation of people who are oppressed and crushed by human structures as, in fact, they historically are. What is at stake here is not an angry God, but the experience of a hard and oppressive world. The concept of an "angry father" was very meaningful in that Victorian time; patriarchy truly carries oppression.

Then the text mentions that "the whole world is thrilled with hope." There is a contrast between the concept of original sin, and the world of hope in salvation and liberation. And the first verse ends with the image of a kneeling and enslaved people waiting for liberation.

When we get into the second part, we realize the harshness of its message. So harsh indeed that, in many churches, the parish priests refused and today still refuse to have it sung. For them it sounds too much like a revolutionary song. The verse emphasizes the distance again, with the concepts of "chiefs," of "king," or "powerful," of "pride," "boldness," of the day that belongs to the powerful while the night belongs to both Christ and the poor. Christ — and thus God — is identified with humility, with the crib, and the powerlessness of a child. And the verse ends with the image of the powerful having to bend their head in the face of that humility. After this analysis, it becomes obvious that such a text could not have been generated in an environment of solidarity with those in power.

The third verse speaks of liberation. "The Redeemer has broken all bonds." What is at stake goes far beyond a merely "spiritual" salvation. "The earth is free" (that is, "the earth" and not only "the heaven"). "He sees a brother where there only

was a slave. Love unites those who were together in chains."
No more do people kneel, like slaves; they stand up. In 1847,
this obviously referred to the working class and to solidarity
among them. It is not difficult to understand why some social
groups did not want such a song sung at Christmas. It carries
a subversive theology. And when it says that the people, now
standing up, can see a brother where there was only a slave,
the rich were rightly disturbed. And Jesus is represented as
the one who was truly in solidarity with the oppressed, and
who died because of that.

This canticle has not been written in just any kind of environment. Even its limitations as a typical sexist song can be related
to the class and the civilization that produced it. And it is then
easier to understand how it has always been a stumbling block.
The rich and the powerful wanted (and still want) it eliminated
from Christmas eve, while the people have always succeeded
in getting it back, despite the priests' most often agreeing with
the well-to-do. For the priests, the main objection always has
been that such an almost revolutionary song does not fit with
Jesus' message. But is that correct? Let us probe the Gospel
with respect to this question.

The Magnificat

As in the Christmas song we analyzed previously, the Magnificat plays with the concepts of distance and of "up and down."
It begins by saying that the individual can be "up": "My spirit
exults in God my Savior." But that happens to the lowly handmaid. She will be blessed by all generations. The Magnificat
thus is structured by images of reversed situations: a humble
woman (that is, belonging to the dominated part of our patri-
archal society) is exalted.

The fifth verse is a very hard one; despite spiritual interpretations, it does not suggest a quiet God who avoids societal and
historical conflicts. On the contrary, the God whom Mary's spirit

magnifies or reflects, "has shown the power of his arm, he has routed the proud of heart, he has pulled down princes from their thrones, and exalted the lowly. The hungry he has filled with good things, the rich sent empty away." Such a text would not need any commentary if it were not often interpreted in a merely spiritual and psychological way. Similarly, when the canticle goes on to proclaim: "He has shown the power of his arm," it is indeed power and force that are being addressed. And the princes are dispersed and pulled from their thrones, while the humble — the servants, the slaves, the exploited, the oppressed — are exalted. The canticle not only says that the hungry will be fed, but it adds that the rich will be sent away empty. Such a text, at the center of the Gospel message, challenges all those who claim that the Gospel only speaks of a merely spiritual experience. On the contrary, the poem almost seems to stem from a "class-struggle" approach. Indeed, the Magnificat is very open to economic dimensions (the rich end up empty), the political dimensions (the princes are pulled down from their thrones) and the ideological dimensions (the lowly handmaid — a servant and woman — is exalted). When this text is not spiritualized, it truly amounts to a subversive poem, threatening the establishment. We thus find in it some of the accents we noticed in the "Minuit Chritiens"; it could also look like a revolutionary song.

The Final Judgment

When, in his Gospel, Matthew pictures the final judgment, he is emphasizing the criteria that, according to the Good News, determine what it means to follow Jesus. The scene shows the Son of Man separating the sheep from the goats. The criterion used is expressed well in the question of the "saints": "Lord, when did we see you hungry and feed you? Or thirsty and give you drink? When did we see you a stranger and make you welcome; naked and clothe you; sick or in prison and go to see you?" And the king will answer: "I tell you solemnly, insofar as you did this to one of the least of the brothers or sisters of mine, you did it to me" (Mt 25:37-40). Here the religion of the oppressed speaks of solidarity; it shows the Son of Man identifying with the poor. When it is not perverted into an opiate of the people, the religion of the oppressed does face social injustices and sees there a special presence of God. As Don Helder Camara has said, "Those who are finally aware of the injustices caused by the unjust distribution of wealth, if they are slightly human, will listen to the protest — unspoken or violent — of the poor. The protest of the poor is indeed the voice of God."

Is Christian Faith a Religion of the Oppressed?

Considering some sections of the Gospel — as the Magnificat or the Beatitudes — it becomes obvious that Jesus' religion — the religion that he practiced and preached — can be correctly seen as a religion of the oppressed. This is not surprising if one remembers the necessary influence of Jesus' lifestyle on his thought: He was the leader of a relatively marginal band, at odds with the establishment and in clear solidarity with all the rejected and crushed.

Actually, it is one of the oldest texts of the Christian Scriptures, the hymn in Paul's Epistle to the Philippians, that gives one of the clearest representations of Christianity as a religion of the oppressed. It conveys an image of God that is obviously related to social, economic, and political imagery. "His state was divine (Jesus seems to have a "class condition" that makes him equal to God), yet he did not cling to his equality with God (here again the relation of Jesus is described in categories relevant to sociopolitical analysis; every person — especially those having significant privileges — inevitably meets the question of either holding on to the privileges or sharing them in solidarity with those who are poor). But he empties himself to assume the condition of a slave (here is the solution by Jesus to the question of the defense of privileges: solidarity with those who are "least," the slaves). And being as all people are, he was humbler yet, even to accepting death, death on a cross (not any kind of death but a death related to the condition of the humblest and of the outcast). But God "raised him high and gave him the name, above all names, so that all beings in the heavens, on earth and in the underworld should bend the knee at the name of Jesus and that every tongue should acclaim Jesus Christ as Lord, to the glory of God the Father" (Philippians 2:6-11). The end of this hymn sounds very similar to the Magnificat: the glorification of Jesus is related to giving up his privileges and entering into solidarity with those who share the condition of slaves.

The image of God conveyed through this hymn is that of a God who could have remained outside our human crises, but who chose not to do so, in order to be committed by taking sides in human history. It is through that solidarity of God that God's glory in Jesus becomes fully manifest. It is thus not difficult to see that the Christian God is not the God of the powerful who governs the universe from a throne. And, as we will see below, neither is it the God of the middle class who tends to keep out of conflicts. The Christian God is in solidarity with the oppressed and is involved in their lives ... to the point of being executed on the cross as an outcast.

This religion of the oppressed can, however, be quite ambiguous. It can turn out to exalt one social class as an elect group, chosen in this case because of poverty. Such a religion may have many messianic overtones, promoting the liberation of the oppressed only to make of them a new privileged group. Obviously that was not the aim of Jesus, even if it was the objective of several of his disciples and also of the people who, finally disappointed in Jesus, gave him up to be crucified.

The Religion of the Middle Class

Middle classes can be defined as social groups that, with respect to those who have power and those who do not, are in an ambiguous position. Middle classes receive enough privileges in the socio-economic system to want to oppose any deep revolutionary change. Lower middle classes, for example, dream of upward mobility and so accept the system mainly as it is. Upper middle classes enjoy such a level of economic welfare that working more to receive more money is no longer appealing to them. But at the same time they have the accurate feeling that they do not have much to say in society. Engineers, middle managers, even doctors and other liberal professions often do not feel that they are really powerful in society. In general, it can be argued that while middle classes do not have much social clout, they enjoy enough privileges to prevent them from being *too* upset about what is going on in society. At the same time, in industrialized countries, these classes — especially the self-employed — work hard, feel that they are heavily taxed, and are exploited. But that does not lead them to revolt; they just become alienated and often bitter. Facing this socio-economic condition, they often withdraw into a dual existence. On the one hand, they carry out their professional life or their work; on the other hand, they seek rewards in their privatized personal or family life (imagine a cottage in the country, a house in the suburbs, or a cozy apartment). Middle classes often withdraw either into their work or into their private lives; they seldom get very involved in politics or in public life. What they expect most from the state and city hall is only that they would not disturb the life they have.

From such a position, middle classes have produced a specific ideology with respect to conflicts. For a middle class person, it is usually scandalous to be involved in a conflictual situation unless the individual person decided to be involved. Middle classes often dream of a world where other people would never organize a strike, where unions would only be there when the individual wants it, where you would not be touched by international crises, where no economic recession could ever condition our way of life. Such an ideology corresponds to the social situation of people who have enough privileges to be able to get out of any immediate conflict. For example, citizens of certain nations — like the NATO countries — if they happen to be in another country where there are political riots or war, can always expect some helicopters sent by their government to evacuate them. For such privileged people it becomes almost an axiom that they never have to be involved, unless they want to.

These middle class attitudes differ from those of the powerful who are not afraid to become involved in conflicts, but who also know that most often they will be protected from their worst consequences. And, as far as the lower classes are concerned, they know they do not have any power to decide in which societal conflicts they will be involved. The poor are aware that, when there is unemployment, depression, riots or wars, they will endure much suffering; they know it is part of their condition.

The Prayer Attributed to Francis of Assisi

The social condition of the middle class seems to be apparent in the prayer for peace that is generally attributed — incorrectly — to Saint Francis of Assisi. The origin of this prayer is not very clear, but it seems to have been composed in Normandy, France, in the bourgeois milieu that surrounded the Carmel of Lisieux.[3] (To have a better idea of the kind of spirituality of these groups, let us remember that they felt it appropriate to edit the autobiography of St. Therese of Lisieux because they did not think the text edifying enough, but too deviant, too "human" and too "realistic.")

Here is the text: "Lord, make me an instrument of your peace. Where there is hatred, let me sow love; where there is injury, pardon; where there is disagreement, unity; where there is error, truth; where there is doubt, faith; where there is darkness, light; and where there is sadness, joy. O Divine Master, grant that I may not so much seek to be consoled as to console; to be understood as to understand; to be loved as to love. For it is in giving ourselves that we receive; in forgetting ourselves

that we find ourselves; it is in forgiving that we are forgiven,
and it is in dying that we are born to eternal life."

This prayer is very inspirational and it can be prayed meaningfully. But it also carried ambiguities — which do not take
away its meaningfulness. (Actually, it would be as ambiguous
to want to avoid ambiguity entirely and to be a purist to the
point of being afraid of speaking. However, it can be very enlightening to examine the ideologies carried through this
prayer.)

Let us begin by considering that here we are facing another
milieu and other psychologies than those at the origin of the
"Minuit Chritiens." It is an entirely different social and mental
universe. First, there is no image speaking of the world as a
whole. We are confronted with a worldview where questions
arise mainly through individual thinking. And this can be a
hallmark of privatized subculture, since not every subculture
sees the individual as the center of the discourse. Thus, this
prayer witnesses to a great concern about that "I" live, what
"I" do, with a touch of psychologizing introspection and anxiety.[4]
This is typical of a "bourgeois" culture.

When we consider the image of Jesus implicit in this prayer,
we discover a Jesus who would like a world where everything
would be *harmonious*. The prayer gives a priority value to peace,
love, pardon, unity, and does not recognize conflict. In such a
context, people will feel uneasy if they want to fight for something. After having prayed such a prayer, it becomes difficult
to think, "I am involved in some conflict and I believe I should
fight till the end." The ambiguity of this prayer relates to the
fact that nobody would ever dream of being "against" peace,
love, pardon, reconciliation. Yet, at the global level, the message
can be very ambivalent. Sometimes interpersonal understanding and pardon is not enough to cope with systemic issues. The
world from which this prayer comes is a universe where people
are respectable, are nice to one another, but where conflicts
are not mentioned. It is a world supposed to be sufficiently well

organized so that there is no need to think about any kind of radical change.

Also related to this kind of mentality, some components of the prayer call for some psychological analysis. What does it mean for people to affirm that it is more important to console than to be consoled, to understand than to be understood, to love than to be loved? Such an approach to life finally amounts to the denial of the importance of receiving. This perspective amounts to promoting a denial of the self. One can then wonder what place is left for the most important feature of Christian life: to let oneself be loved by God and by others. The language of the prayer raises questions at two levels. At the theological level the question is: "How is such a representation compatible with Christian traditions? If God has loved us first, is it in forgiving that we receive forgiveness?" And at the psychological level: "What is the effect of these religious images that emphasize that people should give rather than receive?" The prayer seems to refer to the universe of charity of the well-to-do with its alienations; it promotes a generosity that looks admirable but which includes many ambiguities.

This analysis does not take away the value of this prayer that expressed what the middle classes felt (and still feel) in the society they have helped to build. What I said does detract from the meaning and the importance of promoting peace and of sometimes accepting to give without receiving. But it is quite interesting to become aware that such a prayer stems from a context quite different from the one of St. Francis. When this prayer is compared with his Canticle of the Sun, it becomes obvious that the authors are not the same.

As many Christians no longer feel at ease with the language of that prayer attributed to Francis of Assisi, here is an alternative text. I do not claim that this would be a "good" one, while the other should be rejected. I only invite readers to examine how different are these two prayers for peace, and how their differences indicate that the way we pray speaks of the way we see society.

Lord, make us instruments of your peace:
That we could help love emerge when hate submerges
  everything;
That, in our conflicts, we could meet our enemies with
  tenderness;
That we could find our way among our feelings of love and hate,
  of anger and acceptance, and finally live through forgiveness;
That we could listen to those who cry out in their suffering,
  and could recognize how similar to them we are;
That, in place of using slogans, we seek for more information
  and spread it;
That, in place of repeating the clichés of our culture, we
  come together to analyze what is happening around us;
That we raise up trust where doubt erodes life;
That we shake hands with the foreigner and open our door to
  the refugee;
That where there is despair we let hope grow;
That we bring joy where there is sadness;
That we listen to what others know and share what we know;
That, as it is never possible to see things with absolute
  certainty, we assume our responsibilities, accepting the
  ambiguities they involve;
That we participate in the organization of strikes with the
  exploited;
That we share our bread with the poor, and we oppose
  ideologies which give absolute priority to economic growth;
That we not cling to our privileges, but, while enjoying what we
  have received, still be in solidarity with the powerless;
Lord, that we accept to be sometimes consoled and sometimes
  alone, and teach us to be consoling for others;
That we accept to be sometimes welcome and sometimes
  rejected, but always trying to understand;
That, when there is no longer any other just way, we not be
  afraid of the guerrilla's path, asking together for
  mercy, while trying to step down the spiral of violence;
That the conscientious objector receive his or her place among

us, and that the unemployed not have to build warheads
to have a job;
That everyone accept to be loved, and that everyone love,
because it is when sharing, that everyone receives,
forgiving and accepting to be forgiven, that the kingdom
of forgiveness comes;
That we live and celebrate the sun, the sky, the earth, love
and forgiveness, and meet with trust our sister death, as
it is through her that we are born to eternal life.

Color Us Incarnation

After having analyzed how ambiguous the religion of the
middle class is, typical of this social class, yet filled with life
and hope for life, is "Color Us Incarnation."[5] The poem begins
by what can be seen as a description of the middle class mentality: "Measure if you must, Lord, but we can tell you now
that you will find a strange mixture of common men. A few
among us are good men. Some are evil, who bear your name.
But most are never either, like most men, most places. We are
builders, trowels in hand, but guns loaded, loosely holstered.
Some of us are here for love of you and every brother, most out
of restless curiosity, for want of a better temple." And then,
the poem describes these people of the "middle": "We are men
of moderation in both virtue and vice, which is to say we maintain a place neutrality. We have an allergy to risk. We don't
often fail, but then we don't often try, which is only common
sense. We are a safety-first people. We are finger-nail clip-
pers...."

But in its second part, the poem expresses the prayer and
the hope of the middle class when it is open to the Spirit: "If
truly we are your people, color us incarnation: Out of the slimy
mud of the original chaos you brought meaning and creation.
Out of confused Babel folk you brought a Pentecost speaking,
loud shouting people of joy. Out of us surely you can do it all
again, drab or no. Take our commonness, our curiosity, our

restlessness, our indecision, our neutrality, our musty moderation...." "...Give us safety last, riskability. Make us wild with
you enough at times to be taken for mid-morning drunks...."

Such a text — as well as the parable of the pharisee and the
publican (because pharisees were very much like good middle-
class people!) — is enough to show that the middle class can
also enter the Kingdom ... but not in any kind of way!

DISCUSSION QUESTIONS
1. What are the three levels of conditioning religion that are
distinguished in this chapter?

2. What are, according to this chapter, the characteristics of
the religion of the ruling classes? Find examples in some religious texts. Examine the positive and the ambiguous aspects of
such a religion.

3. Do the same for the "religion of the oppressed."

4. Can a case be made to argue that Christianity is a religion
of the oppressed? How does this influence the representations
of the Christian God?

5. Analyze, as in question 2, the religion of the middle classes.

6. Show how the concept of "eschatological reservation" can be
used to analyze the way in which class condition influences
religion without reducing religion to a class ideology.

[1]Mary Douglas, *Natural Symbols* (Pantheon Books, New York, 1982).

[2]Actually, minorities when they build up counter powers and cultures can use
a discourse and assume attitudes very similar to those of the ruling classes.

[3]Cf. Kajetan Esser, O.F.M.: *Die opuscula des hl Franziskus von Assisi,* Neue
textkritische Edition (1976), p. 54.

[4]The affirmation of the "ego" in the middle classes is often ambivalent. It rarely
is open and frank outside of the privatized and psychologized domain of emo-
tional life. People of the middle classes seem to value the individual very much

but, at the same time, do not easily accept public self-affirmation. All this is related to the social ambivalence of the middle class as described in the beginning of this section.

[5]Taken from *Tender of Wishes* by James Carroll, Newman Press, 1969. The date explains why this poem used sexist language.

17
CHRISTIAN ETHICS

One of the most difficult questions that has to be faced in theology is whether there is a specifically Christian ethics. And, if the answer is yes, then another question comes: "What is it?" This issue can be considered from several points of view. For some, a Christian ethics means that Christians have special norms to fulfill in order to be good people in the eyes of God. For others, the concept of Christian ethics means that, through revelation, Christians know norms or guidelines that other people do not necessarily know even if they are applicable to every human being.

I will consider this subject in a different way from either of these approaches. It is clear that if we accept justification by faith, we do not see ethics as a code of norms or a condition of acceptance by God. Beginning from the obvious fact that a person speaking of ethics is an agent of social and individual action, I will address myself to the questions of its meaning and its relationship with the message of Jesus.

If we think of any theory of ethics as a way of influencing human behavior, our considerations have to be situated in the complete framework of society. In human society, people do not enjoy the freedom of the children of God. On the contrary, they are oppressed by various institutions, ideologies, taboos and other people. They are told what their behavior should be. Into such a situation, Christ has come as a liberator. He frees those whom he meets from the curse of having to obey rules that have become more important than human beings.

And that poses an important question for the Christian who speaks about ethics. Will our statements reinforce the alienations in society or will they, on the contrary, help people to discover the love of God and the freedom of those God loves?

That point of view is almost the opposite of what the teaching of morality often is: the presentation of a set of norms which a person must observe in order to be acceptable. That is why some theologians have said that Christian faith is almost an anti-ethics. It is just the opposite of an oppressive teaching of morality. It is a message of liberation.

The Christian message sets people free but, as St. Paul stresses, it is important to avoid returning into slavery; and that is possible in several ways. One of these would be to so hold to one's freedom that one's life would be devoted to its defense; then, paradoxically, people who are absorbed in defending their freedom become enslaved by what they fear to lose. Another way to get back to slavery would be to act so that others would not be free. That would force people to defend themselves and would finally prevent them from being justified through faith or trust. On the contrary, those who are freed will act as freed persons, and according to the Good News, that means that they will love people as Jesus did. Consequently, as following Jesus implies a certain attitude towards life, we can speak of Christian ethics. It is a way of explaining in the light of the Gospel and the Christian tradition what a Christ-like love can be in a particular society. From that point of view, guidelines for human action can be drawn. As a result of their origins in Jesus, they can be called Christian ethics to distinguish them from guidelines which originate from traditions, philosophies, religions or cultures.

Thus when we speak about Christian ethics, we do not mean that there is a special content in that ethics, but we recognize that like any other ethical thought it comes from a specific cultural background, namely, Christian tradition. This background has to be specified if we want to know what we are speaking about. Christian ethics is, therefore, a reflection on human individual and social behavior that refers to the teaching of Jesus Christ as it has been understood by his followers.

Obviously then, Christian ethics is not given once and for all. According to their particular social, cultural and political situation, the ethical reflection of Christians will be modified. I do not believe in the possibility of a completely ahistorical and acultural ethics. Every ethical thought has its roots in some culture, and in that sense I do not speak either of a natural ethics. What is usually called natural ethics stems from a cultural way of considering the concept of nature.

Let us now say something (obviously from a particular point of view) about the impact of Christian faith on the individual and collective behavior of people. Let us investigate what could be the main lines of a Christian ethics today.

It seems to me that the first thing to be stressed is justification by faith. Through that concept, the priority of God's love over human response (God loves us first) is emphasized and we come to understand that God creates us so that we can decide for ourselves what to do with our own lives. Human beings are thus created to be free, not to be forced to ask for permission about what to do with their lives. That is why any kind of ethical teaching which would reinforce the oppressions to which people are subjected does not stem from the Christian message. In the Gospel you will find protest by Jesus against ethical or legalistic approaches that subjugated people, especially the poor, to the ideologies of the dominant.

Then it is also obvious that Christian ethics is an ethics of love. That does not mean that love is a commandment as people usually speak of commandments. It is more appropriate to say that it is a kind of "recommendation" or "desire" that Jesus has left to his followers. People indeed cannot be ordered to love; they can only be invited to love. Now, according to the Gospel, there is a twofold commandment — to love God and one's neighbor. And, as St. John stresses, the love of neighbor is the only touchstone to test the love of God.

But the Christian message goes further because to speak of loving one's neighbor without specifying who is that neighbor is void of content. That is why Jesus makes clear, especially in the parable of the Good Samaritan, that the neighbor is the person to whom we have decided to be a neighbor, and that there is no limit imposed. That is contrary to norms in many cultures where only relatives or members of the same clan or nation are considered to be neighbors. For Jesus, there is no *a priori* limitation. Everybody can be our neighbor. Because of that, Christians and the Christian community have always tried to reach out to strangers, to the poor, to the oppressed and to the rejected, in order to be their neighbors. There is in the Gospel a definite indication by Jesus that it is only when the poor and the oppressed are freed that the Kingdom is here.

The Gospel definitely recognizes that there is a difference between the oppressor and the oppressed, and it takes sides with the oppressed. The Good News is addressed to them. For the rich, it is impossible to enter the Kingdom unless they share with the poor.

These seem to be the main lines by which Jesus and his followers interpreted ethics. Jesus does not speak about fulfilling many norms, nor does he say that behaviors are indifferent to his Good News. He calls people to love. But that invitation is not compulsory, and there are no strings attached to the love he has for people. However, it would be inconsistent for people who call themselves by his name and who claim to be his followers not to try to liberate their sisters and brothers from all kind of oppressions or blind taboos. That is why Christians feel they are called to struggle for the political, ideological or eithical liberation of mankind. That is also why it is important for the Christian community to get involved in the political arena on the side of the poor and the oppressed. To do so in a meaningful and effective way, a careful social analysis is needed.[1]

Christian ethics cannot be given exact expression in the manner of the ethics of the decalogue. In the Christian tradition
and especially in the Gospel of Matthew, the Beatitudes replace
the proclamation of the Ten Commandments, but the
Beatitudes do not have the same structure as the Commandments. They are a way to happiness; and that happiness or
blessed life is the desire and the hope of God for people "that
they would have joy and would have it completely," as John
says. But if Christians truly live according to the Beatitudes
and the Commandments of love, they will make an important
political impact on society. That is why Christian ethics has
always threatened dominant groups who prefer a more repressive ethics which they can use to protect their privileges. And
this is why Jesus considered it more than likely that his disciples would be persecuted, as a consequence of their liberating
activity. Thus Christian faith, even if it cannot be identified
with any ethical system, is not indifferent toward ethics.

Finally, it is important to remember that Christian ethics
does not give particular answers to any of the human problems.
Anybody reading the Gospels will note that new solutions have
to be found in new situations. It is not fitting to put new wine
into old wineskins. Thus it is impossible to decide in an abstract
way what would be the right behavior according to the heart
of Jesus today. Moreover, it is impossible to find pat answers
to our frequently messy human problems. That is clearly
explained in the parable of the wheat and the weeds. There
Jesus says that the Kingdom of God is comparable to a field
in which good wheat and bad weeds are growing together. The
servants are always tempted to part one from the other. But
that is impossible because people would pull out the wheat
while taking away the weeds. The master of the harvest recom-
mends letting both grow together. That is the human condition.
We never know exactly what is wheat and what is weed. Our
temptation is to want to get rid of any kind of ambiguity instead
of living with it until the moment when the weeds and the
wheat have grown enough to be distinguishable.

That again could be a guideline for Christians. The Kingdom of God is alive and filled with ambiguity; it will be impossible to distinguish fully at this point what in the end will be considered good and what finally will be considered as leading nowhere but to death.

Such an acceptance of ambiguity in one's life is impossible for those who are convinced that they must work to be justified. They have to be sure that the wheat will be separated from the weeds. Justification by works demands such answers and, in their absence, produces anxiety. But those who believe in the love of God can have the patience of letting situations grow with ambiguity so that love can also grow. They know that they are accepted with their ambiguity. If they completely believe in love, anxiety and fear will be completely cast away, as John states in his Epistle. That absence of fear is another criterion of a true Christian ethics. It liberates people from anxiety and allows them to be involved in the liberation of others.

DISCUSSION QUESTIONS

1. Why do some theologians say that Christianity is almost an "antiethics"?

2. In which sense does this chapter accept the notion that there is a Christian Ethics?

3. Give some traits of the Christian traditions with respect to ethics.

4. Why has Christian ethics always been threatening to "law and order" mentalities?

5. How, looking at the Gospel, would you answer people who believe that there are pat answers to messy ethical issues?

6. How would you relate Christian ethics and fear?

[1]On that topic, cf. Joe Holland and Peter Henriot, *Social Analysis: Linking Faith and Justice,* Orbis Books, 1983.

18
LIBERATION ETHICS AND IDEALISM[1]

Liberation theologies provide a framework for serious reflection about systemic issues. But some liberation theologians, while urging social change, foster a guilt-inducing process which actually prevents both personal and social change. The tendency to moralize individual life is thus simply transposed into moralizing collective issues. Absolute search for justice can even sometimes become oppressive. The content of normative ethics is changed but the same guilt-inducing attitudes remain.

This chapter is concerned with the construction of a "liberation ethics" which goes beyond the mere transposition of idealistic moral philosophy to a new set of issues.[2] It deals with meaning of ethical principles and of sin, while constructing an ethics based on historical accounts of liberation. Interestingly, this approach is consonant with the "different voice" of women in ethics, as it has been analysed by scholars like Carol Gilligan.[3]

The Shortcomings of Idealistic Ethics

The current approach in regard to ethics is usually "idealistic." That means that certain images, concepts, ideals and principles are assumed, which are supposed to determine how one is to act. Of course, these ideal principles do not directly dictate what should be done. But, according to idealists, these principles are able to inspire a practice through the mediation of correct reasoning using rational and empirical evidence. Such an approach is exemplified in the moral philosophy of Lawrence Kohlberg.[4] For him, the apex of ethical development consists of letting one's existence be inspired by general and universal principles such as love, justice and human dignity. Popular ethics also relied heavily on an idealistic perspective; when someone says: "This is not truly love," that person refers implicitly to a general and ideal image of love.

A first criticism of idealism stems from philosophy and social sciences. It consists of questioning the origins and conditioning of general principles as well as the biases of rational or empirical analysis. The theory of ideologies emphasizes that ideal images and mental structures are the products of social groups. When someone claims to be directed by a principle of justice, an ideological critique will examine how this idea of justice is connected to a specific social group or class. Far from being universal, any idea of justice can be traced to particular social origins. To be inspired by a principle of justice may amount finally to being guided by a representation which has been culturally produced in a given society and/or social class. We are sometimes reluctant to recognize this type of conditioning when principles related to justice or love are involved. But the theory of ideological conditioning may become clearer if we consider concepts such as what it means to be a man or to be a woman. In our culture it has become obvious that the images of masculinity and femininity are socially produced. To be directed by them will not lead to greater universality, but rather to deeper implication in a particular historical and social conditioning. It is possible to trace the same dynamics of conditioning with general concepts such as justice, love, responsibility, commitment, honesty, human dignity, etc.

Analogous reasoning may be applied to concrete analyses and to their empirical support. Many moralists claim that their argumentation relied upon a universal rationality and that they speak of "things as they are." There again the theory of ideologies as well as cognitive psychology challenges the so-called direct approach of "reality." It can be shown that our analyses never depend upon "things as they are" or upon a universal rationality, but upon a certain interpretation and a certain construction of the world. On that account, it is necessary to recognize that the arguments of moralists (and of any people seeking to justify their attitudes) are relative. They are conditioned by human psycho-biology; by cultural representations shared within a society, a subgroup or a social class; and finally by personal history. This conditioning does not mean that rationality and ethical analyses are not important. It simply emphasizes the incorrectness of giving them a status of pure objectivity or complete universality.

A second objection to the idealistic approach of ethics stems from a specifically Christian and theological point of view. An idealistic approach leads moralists to direct people to behave according to abstract and general principles. Thus, for many, the most important criterion in morality is to ask oneself if what one does corresponds to a particular definition of what is "good" or "evil." Similarly, we have seen how, for Kohlberg, the maturity of ethical development consists of being inspired by general principles and of reaching decisions in relation to them. These perspectives, which many assume to be Christian, actually deviate from Christian traditions. As a matter of fact, according to biblical traditions, the ethical meaning of our existence is not determined in relation to general and abstract principles. It is related to a person: God, and for Christians, to God incarnated in Jesus Christ and executed as an outcast. There is a deep difference between deciding about one's life in relation to ideas or in relation to a personal and historical presence.

The theory of ideologies can shed further light on this difference. This theory suggests that abstract concepts of "good" and "evil" usually function so as to conceal conflicts between persons and groups. For example, the statement: "Adultery is evil" masks another more concrete message, such as, "If you continue to fool around with my wife, you will get my fist in your face."

Abstract ideological reasoning often veils underlying interpersonal or collective conflicts. The biblical perspective, on the contrary, refers to interactions of human beings with one another and with God. The Christian God is even identified with specific people such as the widow, the orphan, the stranger, the oppressed. God is involved with people, making a covenant with them, sometimes in conflict with them, but always in personal relationship.

The Historical Character of Ethical Concepts

In order to go beyond idealistic morals, we have to develop a historical moral philosophy and see how rationality functions in its ethical arguments. To situate such a historical ethics in a broader context, we can refer to several philosophies: to Maruice Blondel (especially in his *Action*,[5] 1893); to phenomenologists; to Nietzsche (especially to his treatment of reason and science). Among social scientists I would refer to *The Social Construction of Reality* of Peter Berger and Thomas Luckman,[6] to the concept of "imaginary institution" of Cornelius Castoriadis,[7] as well as to the current of cognitive psychology. In the Christian traditions, we can draw upon the work of the nominalists of the Middle Ages who reject the notion of an ideal essence of things in order to emphasize how concepts are constructed. In a rather consistent way, the nominalists do not speak of a confrontation with "natural ends or ideals" but with God; concomitantly, they emphasize human commitment.

The historical approach presupposes that our general concepts such as "masculinity," "femininity," "friendship," "responsibility," "human dignity" or "justice" are historically constructed. Epistemological, sociological, psychological analyses converge in stating that it is impossible to claim that one speaks "of things as they are." We always use culturally produced interpretative representations. Concepts receive their meanings from stories which relate to and interpret events according to our culture, as well as to specific individual contexts. For example, the term "to be responsible" refers to a series of cultured stories which speak of the manner in which people or groups have behaved in a "responsible way." It is the same for "masculinity" or "feminity" or "love" etc. Concepts are like a kind of shorthand used to designate a series of stories. In a non-idealistic approach "eternal ideas" are of a historically situated culture. Moreover, these stories vary according to the social position of the group which produces them.

The stories connected to concepts help people to situate themselves and thus to tell their own story. When, for example, a girl says that she is in love, that means that, on the one hand, she recounts her personal history through the tales of love which are told in her culture, and that these tales (culturally acquired and socially determined) become clearer for her because of her own experience. Thus there is a kind of dialectic relation between the tales present in the culture and people's own stories. (For Christians, such a connection is made between their story and the story of Jesus. The Gospel tells about Jesus' actions and people read their own lives in the light of these stories. This could be the meaning of the traditional concept of living in one's existence the mystery of the life of Jesus.) Stories people hear — whether they be those of Jesus, or Ghandi, or Martin Luther King, of the crossing of the Red Sea, of a revolution, of the workers' movement, of stories of those we approach negatively like those of Hitler or of Sade — are calls which finally help people to tell their personal and collective tales.

In this construction, ethics is then no longer seen as deduced from eternal concepts. Human decisions are thought through not in an effort to comply with universal reason but rather in a dialogue with particular stories. Ethical reflection thus appears to be a historical production determined by numerous conditions. Ethics no longer claims to be an absolute and universal discourse, rather it refers to a relative objectivity. It cannot distinguish absolutely the good grain from the tare (at least not before the definitive eschatological coming of the Kingdom). However, rational discourse with its relative criteria and its empirical foundation helps people to discern the signs of the times, the stories that speak to us and the calls that we want to utter or that we want to listen to. Rational discussion then takes place somewhere between skepticism and certitude. This is perhaps our human condition: human beings are unable to say the last word about anything, and nevertheless rational discussion is extremely relevant in order to relate our own story. Perhaps it is by accepting the impossibility of ultimately telling what is "good" and "evil" that morals can escape from a totalitarian or a paternalistic oppression of persons and of collectivity.

Many, to the left as well as to the right, lean towards idealism and hesitate to recognize that our ethical arguments are social constructs and thus relative. Even many liberation theologians are tempted to claim that they have absolutely determined that Christians must get involved in revolutionary change. By thus refusing nominalistic or phenomenological epistemologies, these ethicists remain idealistic (asnd there are even idealistic interpretations of Marx). They prefer to claim that ethics speaks of "things as they are" and is finally able to determine what is "good" and "evil." This subtly reintroduces a deductive ethics, even if most ethicists recognize — at least in theory — that perceptions and reasonings are socially and psychologically conditioned. Moreover, such idealistic ethics most often reflect the values of the privileged social classes and nations.

To perceive the relative and ideological character of moral reflection by no means implies that one neglects its relevance nor that of reason. Analyses are necessary for clarifying situations, but cannot ultimately determine the mystery of human choices. Practical confrontation with situations, people, groups and structures, can never be reduced to analytical or rational terms. Between our legitimate arguments and our actions there is always a gap. This is the place of the mystical dimension of life which involves trust in self, trust in people and — for believers — trust in God.

Ethicists who hold moral absolute principles often believe they are defending the value of human action. But it could be argued that, in so doing, they neglect some of its dimension. In the idealistic approach when what is "good" has been deduced from principles, people know what they should do. The dimension of personal risk present in human commitment is thus almost obliterated. The human "I" is veiled behind the legitimizing agencies denounced by Nietzsche: morality, science, reason, religion. Yet, every ethical decision has an element of risk. Whatever the sharpness of our analyses, we are never sure of the ultimate meaning of our actions. Trust is thus needed, with its mystical dimension. In theological language, this trust can be related to the doctrine of justification by faith.

Thus when it emphasizes the impossibility of knowing exactly the ethical meaning of our actions, liberation ethics can avoid two stumbling blocks: becoming identified with only one ideology and inducing guilt when we make mistakes. To found such an ethics, however, a prophetic vision of sin, as well as the doctrine of justification by faith, are still necessary.

In a historical approach to ethics, reflection on sin stems from the concrete confrontation with suffering and evil in the history of people. The new awareness begins with hearing the cries of those who experience evil: the widow, the exploited, the oppressed, the raped, the orphan. These cries are a starting point which leads to reflection on human actions and their underlying conflicts. They are then relayed by prophetic voices inviting recognition of the "new sins" revealed by the suffering, anger and sometimes hatred of the oppressed. Prophetic voices, themselves, are followed by the rational elaboration and analysis of moral theories. These steps lead individuals and groups to confess their sin "before God and people," and to convert.

The suffering and cries of the oppressed will have then led to a new awareness of sinfulness as well as a new ethical system or a new ethical rationale. This system is provisionary because it stems ideologically from specific social groups. Later that ethics, when established, will show its partial origins and lead to some kind of oppression. The ethics of private property, for example, while intended to protect the less privileged from the greed of the powerful, has ended protecting that very greed. And the cycle will repeat itself: cries of the newly oppressed, prophetic voices and a new ethical system that can be used to discuss rationally where we stand and with whom we are in solidarity.

Such an approach can save ethics from being just another legitimizing ideology of dominant groups. It is not founded on abstract principles but on concrete situations where evil is met. Abstract principles and reason have their place, important but limited; they are necessary means toward the awareness and confession of sin. But they are also ambiguous social constructs conveying the conscience of particular social groups, usually well-educated and economically developed groups. Moral theology then can take its place in the great tale of "salvation history," that of God laboring among his people against "evil," toward liberation and the kingdom.

Finally, liberation ethics leads to emphasis on another central element of Christian traditions: justification by faith, that is, by trust. If indeed our own value if founded only on the correct choices we could have made, it would be very threatening not to be able to distinguish clearly "good" and "evil" precisely because they implicitly presuppose a justification by works theology. If indeed our reason cannot clearly show us what is to be done, our relying on justification by works becomes unbearable. On the contrary, justification by faith gives people a real freedom that enables them to act. Liberation ethics, when it is so based, opens to mystical commitment based on trust, while at the same time insisting on precise analyses.

DISCUSSION QUESTIONS

1. How is an idealistic ethics defined in this chapter?

2. Give a philosophical criticism of idealistic ethics.

3. Does Christian ethics mainly refer to abstract principles or to living people? What does that imply with respect to idealistic ethics?

4. How do concepts like "good" and "evil" tend to conceal conflictual situations?

5. What is the difference between an ethics that refers to general and universal discourse and an ethics that refers to a relative objectivity?

6. What does it mean to state that a non-idealistic ethics stems from the suffering of the oppressed?

7. How does this chapter approach the philosophy of moral development of Lawrence Kohlberg?

[1]This chapter has been published in *New Blackfriars, 65,* 763, pp 35-41, 1984.

[2]For a more extended study of this topic, of G. Fourez: *Liberation Ethics,* Temple University Press, Philadelphia, PA, 1982.

[3]Cf. Carol Gilligan: *In a Different Voice,* Harvard University Press, Cambridge, MA, 1982.

[4]Cf. Lawrence Kohlberg: *The Philosophy of Moral Development,* Harper & Row, New York, 1981.

[5]Paris 1893. Reprinted by Presses Universitaires de France, Paris, 1950.

[6]Anchor Books, New York, 1967.

[7]*L'Institution Imaginaire de la Société,* Seuil, Paris, 1975.

19
CHRISTIAN VIEW OF CONFLICT

We Christians often have a dream. We dream that it is possible for us to live entirely in a peaceful way. We dream of a harmonious world where all things are clear and where nothing disturbs us. Moreover, we often avoid becoming aware of anything that might challenge our quietude. We do not want to accept the reality that about ninety-five percent of our lives is lived in conflict.

If we wait for the end of conflicts to begin to live fully, it could be that at the end of our life we will discover that we have never truly lived. Our lives would have been spent in trying to establish a situation without struggle and that does not exist. It is important to face the fact that there are conflicts and that we must learn to live through them in a Christian way. After all, it would be strange that as Christians we would not have to experience opposition when Jesus spent much of his public life in conflict with many groups and individuals.

Every evangelist, in his or her own way, tells us about Jesus' struggles, but the Gospel of John relates them more explicitly. He has structured his way of looking at the Good News through Jesus' encounters with the Jews, until he was crucified. If the pattern of this Gospel indicates what Jesus was trying to live, it is important to see how we can live through conflictual situations in a Christian way.

We often avoid conflicts because we fear them. That is under-
standable. When we meet somebody who is either our enemy
or who does not agree with us we sense how much an encounter
with this person could change us. Hence, we often try to avoid
conflicts and struggles for power. Moreover, since most Christians are middle class, one has to take into account the middle-
class ideology that sees as an ideal not to have enemies and to
be nice to everybody (and in doing so middle-class peole most
often just conceal the structural or relational conflicts in which
they are involved).

There are many ways to avoid these tensions and to regress
toward a childish world of false harmony. The first way is to
reject the potential enemy by imagining or believing him or
her to be a bad and unworthy person. That was often the case
when people were called "heretics." An enemy viewed in that
light will only touch the externals of our life and will not
threaten our deepest self. The tension is then relegated to the
periphery of our lives.

Another way of avoiding conflict is to refuse to give our potential enemy the freedom to be different and, instead, to assimilate
the other into our own vision. That is done, for example, when
some theologians call people who refuse to be Christians
"anonymous Christians," deciding that they are really not so
different from Christians. We then decide that others are the
same as ourselves and this assimilation allows us to avoid
facing the differences. This also allows us to avoid confronting
our aloneness before others. Such a tendency can be noticed in
many religious phraseologies where harmony, reconciliation,
unity are emphasized and praised. It is also frequent in some
ways of describing the "ideal" married couple as almost only
one person, completely neglecting the aggressiveness, the tensions and the conflicts. By all these means we often try to
re-establish a harmonious world where differences, struggles
and opposition are not recognized. That is the kind of universe
that, unfortunately, "mother" Church has often presented to

us. But it could well be that, in doing so, we simply enclose ourselves in a narcissistic universe and prevent any true intrusion of God in our lives. Rather than avoiding conflicts, could we see them as an epiphany of God in the world?

In the Bible God is described as the intruder who comes to change the world and who comes as a thief in the night. Actually, that is the way we can experience God in conflicts. The other, our enemy, is like an intruder. When such a person stands before us without wanting to give up, that person forces us to recognize that we can never claim a complete understandiang of what life is all about. That is how, in a conflict, the enemy forces us to give up the attitude of believing we can reduce reality to our categories. We are then forced to give up any claim of possessing an absolute righteousness, and we are ultimately obliged to recognize our finite condition as a created human being. Thus, our enemy forces us to recognize that we are not God and to abandon our God-like and idolatrous claim of absoluteness.

Without enemies everyone would soon yield to some narcissistic idolatry. That is why the experience of conflict can be a deep experience in which God comes as an Other, destroying our idols, and reminding us of our human condition. At the same time, the presence of an enemy forces us to recognize our uniqueness as free persons. When others struggle with us they force us to give our unique response and to take the risk that can lead to the discovery of ourselves as unique persons.[1]

Conflict, then, is an experience where we discover ourselves as people trusting God enough to dare to act, to speak and to think about what we believe in. That special experience brings to us a deep awareness of the human condition. It manifests that we do not have absolute knowledge of our mission in this world. It shows us that we have our own personal answers to the call of God and to the call of others. We discover ourselves as unique persons who have importance for ourselves and also as persons who cannot say that we know everything and that we are everything. That discovery leads us to worship the One who is beyond ourselves and beyond our adversaries: God.

Thus, conflicts are the most privileged ways we can discover who God is. The adversary is always there to save us from our idolatry and at the same time to manifest our response as persons who have to assume responsibility. That is why it is important to avoid eliminating conflicts by assimilating enemies to our own patterns (cf. the "anonymous Christians") or by deciding that they have no value in themselves (cf. the "heretics"). Doing so would avoid conflictual encounters which could be the epiphany of God in our lives. Moreover, we would soon believe that we are the center of the world. These conflicts are even more significant when they happen between believers because their adversaries make their decisions in the name of the same Christ, the same God and the same Gospel. The differences between their stands force the recognition that no one can ever possess God and no one has the only interpretation of the Gospel. There again conflicts save people from idolatry, on the condition, however, that one does not make these conflicts a goal or an absolute in themselves.

Perhaps this is why the special commandment of Christ to love one's enemies has always been the center of Christianity. It is not through peaceful transactions with friends that we meet God on privileged ground. We meet him when we recognize God in conflicts and when we love our enemies. Unfortunately, that commandment of Christ has been split from one sentence into two: one saying "to love everybody," and the other commanding "not to have any enemies." It is obvious that such an understanding completely misses the point. The Gospel says: "love your enemy." It implies that we have enemies, that we do not always agree and that we will perhaps fight to death. At the same time, it invites us to love these enemies as persons who are human as we are and who sometimes even refer to the same Gospel as we do. To love our enemies is mind-blowing. But that commandment can help us to understand who God is. He is beyond and yet in our struggle. We meet God there as the Transcendent when we discover that neither we nor our enemy possess him. In such a situation, by being beyond us, God allows us to discover some unity even between adversaries.

Moreover, in such a conflict, we face the possibility of having to give up our own point of view. We even know that will happen. Thay is why conflict also is a privileged experience of facing the mystery of the death of Christ. He experienced conflict when he was confronted with the Jews and the Sanhedrin. At that point he was one of us — unable to show the reason for the confrontation, whether he was right and what was to lead him to his death. He was alone. Christians experience all of that in conflicts, and through such conflicts, they hope that God's love will become manifested. That is the mystery of the Resurrection.

The preceding analysis of conflicts between individuals can also be applied to the collective tensions of the Christian community. The Christian community, the Church, is tempted to avoid conflicts, just as individuals are. When it yields to that temptation, the Church closes itself and becomes a sect which considers others either the same as itself or as bad and worthless. It refuses, thus, the challenge of strangers or enemies who force it to destroy its idols. That is why it is important for the Church to recognize that it is its enemies who liberate it from its alienation.

According to this analysis, the conflict we experience while loving our enemies is an epiphany of God. A Christian community, thus, is not called to be a nice, innocuous group. When it is, it has lost its meaning and impetus. It is called to recognize the always unexpected God who is revealed to those who love their enemies through the social and collective conflicts of life.

DISCUSSION QUESTIONS

1. Why is there a tendency to avoid conflicts? Explain how the mechanisms of assimilation and of rejection work in that process.

2. Draw from the Bible some images or situations that take conflict into account, instead of hiding or denying it.

3. How are the intruder, the foreigner and the enemy, potential carriers of God's presence?

4. Why is it that without enemies, we could soon become idolatrous? or very narcissistic?

5. How does conflict force us to deal with our uniqueness and our aloneness? How can it be called an Epiphany of God?

6. Analyze the sentence: "Love your enemies?"

7. How can conflictual experience be related to the passion of Christ?

---

[1]It is worthwhile noticing that we have here the basis for a "conflictual" spirituality of marriage. In a couple, the beloved is always also the intruder, the other. Similarly, in any kind of human interaction (at work, in political life, the parish organization, in schools, in home and school meetings), the encounter with others is important to remind us of the relativity of our position.

20
MEASURING AND FORGIVING

Klaus Barbie, the head of the Gestapo in Lyon, France (nicknamed the "butcher of Lyon") has been arrested.... After forty years, should he be punished or forgiven? The Guatemalan Indians, as well as others, having been massacred by whites who clung to their privileges, feel anger and hatred added to their sufferings. Is a discourse on forgiveness in order here, or would it only be a trap set to perpetuate the white people's rule? We can also mention the Blacks of South Africa or people without a country who face similar issues. France can be considered, to a certain point, "reconciled" with Germany after forty years; but what does that really mean? When Sandinistas took over Nicaragua, one of their leaders declared: "Our vengeance will be forgiveness." How can this proclamation go along with the necessity to struggle for keeping what has been achieved by the revolution? Between groups and nations, or when class struggle is concerned, profound and "gut-level" feelings arise because of the struggle against exploitation; this brings anger and hatred towards the oppressor, while solidarity and fraternity unite the oppressed. Is there a place, among all this, for a feeling such as forgiveness? And is this feeling, interpersonal from the outset, appropriate in collective situations? Another issue concerns responsibilities in collective problems. For example, are there some people responsible when there is an economic recession? If nobody is responsible, does forgiveness make any sense? If yes, on what conditions and how is forgiveness meaningful?

177

In interpersonal relationships, people often tell stories about forgiveness, for example, when married couples are concerned. But it is not easy to discern in which cases forgiveness can be seen as leading to growth and in which cases it amounts to a shared trap (or, even more, to a neurotic feeling). When is it meaningful to ask or to grant forgiveness? Conflicts pervade all types of family situations, even the happiest. Whether it be between husband and wife, or parents and children, aggressiveness, or even hate, is part of the family picture. And when there is conflict, the issue of forgiveness is there: how can people live it meaningfully?

Forgiveness, a Hazy Notion

We could go on enumerating situations where people speak of forgiveness. The diversity of these situations points to the fact that the notion of forgiveness, like that of reconciliation, is blurred, and ought to be analyzed each time in a critical fashion, to relate it to a precise context in which it can make sense. The concept takes on a completely different meaning in an interpersonal as opposed to a collective situation; but even within the collective level, the meaning and the effects of the word can vary greatly. When we say that France and Germany have been reconciled, or when we speak about reconciliation between a class of workers and proprietors, the word "reconciliation" doesn't have the same meaning. That's why it is imprudent to speak about forgiveness and reconciliation in a general way, for example, to say that "Jesus Christ came to preach forgiveness under any circumstance." Such a discourse can function as an ideology by helping to conceal differences and conflicts for the benefit of those who defend the established order or disorder. As soon as forgiveness is addressed, people must then be alert so that this discourse is not used for the benefit of any conflicting party. As a consequence, conditions of authenticity for the practice of forgiveness have to be carefully analyzed.

In spite of the difficulties encountered in speaking about forgiveness in general terms, accounts and stories related to the concepts of forgiveness and reconciliation belong to our mental universe and our culture. For Christians, for exampale, the image of remission of a debt (sin) is a very essential part of the Gospel's message. And everyone, willingly or not, produces some discourse on forgiveness. It is, therefore, impossible, in our culture, not to take a stand with respect to stories concerning forgiveness. Everyone, whether individually or collectively, conveys an ethics of forgiveness, even if we find the notion ambiguous. This chapter will analyze some issues at stake when people use the concept of forgiveness.

A World Where Everything is Measured

In both interpersonal and collective situations, it is important to recognize and then analyze different points of view and eventual resulting tensions; furthermore, one must know who crushes and who liberates whom; it is, therefore, necessary to judge *situations* independent of any judgment or opinion concerning the persons involved. All of these analyses constitute "the world of measurement," a world contrary to the dream of a fusional society where people would have complete and harmonious union. In reality, conflicts, exploitation, domination and differences are always part of our universe.

Denying tensions generally amounts to taking sides for one or another confronting party, and most often for the "dominating" one. For example, a teacher, our employer or a dominant partner in a couple, have their interests cared for when people say that the classroom, the factory, or the household should live harmoniously and without too many tensions; this is because they eventually are those in charge of organizing these institutions. As soon as fundamental equality between individual or collective partners doesn't exist, the absence of precise analyses is most often detrimental to the smaller ones. That's

why analyses and law are necessary in every human relationship, as bases for justice; they allow judgment and denunciation
of oppression. Never can a call to forgiveness or reconciliation
neglect this need for analysis and measurement when it wants
to end by producing justice. Experience as much as theoretical
reflection shows indeed that, for the less strong, it is always
dangerous to abandon one's rights for the benefit of "reconciliation" and the good will of the powerful.

Analyses of tensions are thus necessary, but we must also
point out the ambiguities and limits of the "world of measuring."
Of course, accounting of rights, reasons and wrongs can favor
the weak, but often only the strong have the capacity to perform
such "accounting," to appeal to the "world of measurement,"
because they already have access to the means necessary for
asserting their rights. In order to know one's rights, instruction
is necessary. In order to find a way through the labyrinth of
right and wrong one must actually be clever and thus able to
defend oneself. Without some economic, social and juridical
force, "being right" does not help at all. Besides being right,
power is necessary. That is why, in our society, the ethics of
calculation or negotiation of rights is historically connected to
the rising of the middle-class merchant and industrial society.
The issue of measuring is the issue of those who, like La Fon-
taine's ant, feel able to measure everything and thus to justify
their claims. On the contrary, the less privileged social classes
often feel that if they are thoroughly measured, they will always
be found wanting. In the world of the powerful, people do not
like to owe anything to anyone and they try to know exactly
how they can be debt-free. Among the poor, however, people
often show a rather good-natured and cheerful generosity and
they do not measure. Obviously, the poor know that measuring
will never produce an account favorable to them. Justification
through works is an ethics of the "powerful."

In the long run, the world of measure becomes unendurable.
If analysis is necessary to make the rights of the weak conspicu-
ous, to hold only to measuring amounts is to become enclosed

in a sealed universe dominated by the fear of being "measured" and of coming up too short. When measurement becomes an ideal, the result is a terrifying world of coldness and solitude. In order to survive in such a closed universe, many conceal the contradiction of their life and hide their limitations, as did the Pharisee in the parable. Once lived as an absolute, the logic of measurement results in a deadlock and can become a curse: being bound to be always perfect.

The logic of measurement not only leads to cold isolation, but also to violence through the phenomenon of the scapegoat.[1] Social groups and individuals who want to be represented as "just" can do so only if they are able to designate a "guilty" person or group: some individuals, a social class, a nation or a race, who are presented and perceived as the cause of every kind of evil. The unity of groups is built, in this case, on the rejection of the scapegoats, for example, Communists, immigrants, Jews, employers, proletarians, white or black and so forth.

In short, if analysis is necessary to safeguard a place for justice, logic and measurement, pushed to their limits, lead to a dead end. For a married couple, claiming to be right does not resolve the problem of "living together;" in society, every analysis, whether it is Marxist dialectics or Christian theology, always brings with it some elements which will become totalitarian if transformed into an absolute. Something beyond logic is, therefore, necessary; it is then that the subjects of forgiveness, remission of debts and non-measurement make sense.

Forgiveness as Openness

Forgiveness can be defined as a "transgression" of the logic of measurement, a transgression by which the other or others are recognized and accepted beyond conflicts. When the Sandinistas, taking over power, say that their vengeance will be their forgiveness, they deviate from the usual "give and take" situation. With regard to a couple, when one of the partners decides to abandon the defense of "reasons" for forgiving and asking forgiveness, he/she transgresses the rule of calculation of rights and wrongs, with the non-rationality and risk that is then involved.[2] In collective situations, speaking of forgiveness brings similar effects. But as with every transgression, forgiveness instills fear into those who make an absolute of the defense of the established order. The "bourgeois" world, the calculating world and the world which masters analysis (always "scientifically," whether they be from the left or the right) fear the non-rationality related to forgiveness, and will often tend to require a perfect justice before daring to celebrate the meeting and love of human beings. Thus, the motto "no celebration without justice" is ambiguous. On one hand, it can show the danger of replacing the search for justice by a celebration — which would then become a farce. On the other hand, taken literally, this motto leads nowhere; since justice is never complete, there would never be any celebration. This deadlock, connected to the absolutization of analyses, is transgressed by forgiveness; the poor celebrate together when they can.

The world of the poor seems less squeezed by the necessity of "measurement" unless the ethics and ideology of the "strong" have been imposed upon them. Those who lack the feeling of mastering their life can more easily accept and forgive one another, even when it is not logical or at the price of ambiguities that should be denounced. This is the case of a man or woman who accepts his or her partner again without asking for an explanation; or of a worker who, after a difficult social struggle, is ready to fraternize with his or her employer; of a community that offers a place again to someone who has betrayed it; or of someone who welcomes an alcoholic member of the family. All of this seems illogical to the bourgeois ethics, as well as to the ethics of the eldest son in the parable of the Prodigal Son.

All these attitudes stem from the conviction that it is not worth the trouble to measure or to calculate, because we all are limited and measurement will only lead us to be all rejected and condemned. This philosophy of life acknowledges the impossibility of completely mastering evil in our existence. Consequently, we all have a need to be forgiven, individually as well as ccollectively. Although this popular logic sometimes conceals the necessity of analysis, to the point of passively accepting domination or exploitation, it conveys a profound human wisdom.

Christianity and Forgiveness

The Christian message is centered around the notion of forgiveness. Jesus presents an image of a God who forgives, calling people to do the same. The Kingdom he proclaims is just the contrary of cold justice; it is found in the warm tenderness of those who feel accepted in a gratuitous manner that goes beyond all measure. For example, when the adulteress is saved from legal stoning, Jesus suggests that only the person who has never sinned should cast the first stone. The parable of the king who forgives the debt of a servant while the latter demands an integral reimbursement from one of his colleagues conveys the same message: the only unacceptable thing in the Kingdom of God is the refusal of forgiveness and of being forgiven. Finally, the most central words of the "Our Father" are "Forgive us our debts as we forgive our debtors." For Christians, God is not found in the logic of measurement, but in the dynamics of "grace," that is, of the gratuitousness of love. Christian faith is not a religion for the "just" but for the "forgiven." It stems from dynamics contrary to the logic of the scapegoat. For the Christian, there is neither pagan nor Jew, master or slave, man or woman, even if it is necessary to analyze society in using these categories because they disclose significant differences, tensions, and conflicts.

Ambiguities of the Ideologies of Reconciliation

The particular relation of forgiveness to social order and to action toward justice makes it an ambiguous reality.

The first ideological stumbling block comes from the frequent confusion between *forgiveness* and *reconciliation*. We can only speak about reconciliation when the conflict has ended and a new set of social relationships which are experienced as just have been established. Actually, there are on earth only partial reconciliations because justice is never completely achieved. For Christians, reconciliation is eschatology, that is, hope in the final reign of God in history accomplished in its fullness. To speak about reconciliation without specifying its partial character most often amounts to denying the existence of conflicts and thus favoring those who receive privileges from the established order (or disorder). It is generally the party in power who propose *reconciliation;* the oppressed rather wish for a *truce* or for a *liberation.*

Forgiveness does not necessarily imply reconcilation; it is compatible with conflict and the denunciation of injustice. As a word or a gesture which expresses what lies beyond the conflicts, forgiveness recognizes and accepts (or loves) the other party (individual or collective) without suppressing the real antagonism which remains. Forgiveness signifies our acceptance that, in the end, we will die without ever seeing the resolution of numerous conflicts, whether these concern personal situations (for example, with a married couple), or collective tensions, such as class struggles, sexism and so forth. In this perspective, to ask forgiveness does not at all imply, as many think, a confession of being "wrong." Rather it first means acknowledging that, in conflicts, we hurt one another. By asking forgiveness, we ask the other party to accept us in spite of that hurt. This somehow implies admitting we never are entirely right, but not necessarily that we are wrong in the ordinary sense of the word. To ask forgiveness doesn't necessarily mean that we have decided to act otherwise. It can, indeed, happen that we don't see how to come to a more "just" situation even though we desire to live forgiveness. In this light, to forgive implies neither that we are right nor that we are guilty. The dynamics of forgiveness — requested, received and given — introduces, therefore, a certain relativity in conflicts, none of which are ultimate without, however, denying their reality and importance.

The request for forgiveness will, however, only be actual or concrete if we articulate in some way or another the evil in which we share a part; people always ask forgiveness for something in particular. And so do Christians when they confess their sins. However, to so designate evil does not mean that we *ultimately* know what we are guilty of. Even more that does not imply we can *ultimately* measure responsibility. This is why the dynamics of forgiveness cannot be taken for granted in a society influenced by the bourgeois ethic, a society which overestimates individual responsibility and which does not recognize that, everywhere, the wheat still lives with the tare. What we designate when we ask for forgiveness is never clear and can never be completely computed.

In the same way, the relationship — often suggested — between forgiveness and forgetfulness is ambiguous. For many, the only way to forget would be to repress feelings and memories, even though they will probably return in one way or another. If "forgetting" means no longer keeping an account of what has happened, the fact remains that this does not imply a true reconciliation in "justice." And reconciliation does not require forgetting. Rather forgiveness consists in allowing conflicts to be lived in a new atmosphere of openness well described by Louis Lavalle: "The very fault that others have committed against us creates a tighter bond of flesh between us and them, that forgiveness can make spiritual." Forgiveness — and faith in forgiveness — then become a way to live the human story, while refusing to reduce it totally to its conflictual elements.

A last ambiguity in the notion of forgiveness stems from the assimilation of forgiveness in interpersonal and in collective relationships. Indeed, if *I* decide to forgive, I only do this in my own name while it is not easy to know who can speak in the name of a collective group when it forgives. Even if there is a sense of pronouncing words of forgiveness collectively in the name of a community, the question still remains about the legitimacy of the words, a question that is not very relevant when only one person is involved.[3]

Beyond Reasons: the Celebration of Forgiveness

It is impossible to build a "theory" about forgiveness (no more than one can build one on transgression), if, eventually, we assume that such a "theory" should justify forgiveness by some rational analysis. That would amount, indeed, to reducing for-giveness to a component among others in the logic of rights and wrongs; in the end some would be "wrong" or "right," be-cause either they forgive or not. Seen from this perspective, the dynamics of forgiveness would be "co-opted" by reasons. Calling for a rational or ethical harmony born of forgiveness would only give rise to a new established order, which would moreover produce the logic of the scapegoat by designating "good" and "evil." Forgiveness cannot be understood as only a component of interpersonal and social analyses. On the con-trary, it ought to be thought of and lived beyond such rationalities, or at least be a sign of something which cannot be reduced to logic.

To the extent that forgiveness is an opening and a break with respect to rationalities, it stems from another dynamic, and specifically from that of ritual celebrations. Celebrations are moments of pause in existence, through which we can get deeply in touch with what we live more profoundly. They open to many levels of meaning and call for some inspiration, plenitude, new-ness. To celebrate forgiveness is thus, by a kind of ritual mime, to affirm that there is something *beyond* the conflicts and negotiations of life. It is also to proclaim in hope, that what is today the fabric of our tensions (with calculation and negotia-tion) can become a bond of love and tenderness. These "calcu-lations of forgiveness" happen much more often than when people celebrate official and socially recognized rituals; they can be lived through moments of relaxation and tenderness in the simplicity of everyday existence.

The Call to Forgiveness

When we are immersed in a conflict, it is often impossible to perceive anything other than our own desires or the defense of our interests. Unless another voice calls us to ask for forgiveness and to forgive, we could easily become the prisoners of our conflicts. However, the call to forgiveness is ambiguous, even more than forgiveness itself. It can, indeed, be used by one of the confronting parties to strengthen its position in the conflict. How, for example, can we call the blacks and whites of South Africa to forgiveness without recognizing that such a call could reinforce the established disorder? Likewise, in difficult inter-personal relationships, it is not rare that one of the partners would perceive such a call to forgiveness as an invitation to conceal or refuse the reality of the conflict. Who, then, can call to forgiveness and in the name of what or of whom?

In order not to be a trap, a call to forgiveness should come from a recognition of "otherness"; this is necessary so that the call might not be recaptured in the logic of the political or interpersonal conflict. On this point, Christian traditions and their symbolism are suggestive. For them, the only one who can call to forgiveness with full authenticity is the totally "other" of the conflict — God. The Christian God is presented as beyond human history, but engaged in it as well, in order to be able to call us toward *something beyond* the conflicts. God has accepted being in jeopardy in Jesus, to the point of giving up God's own life.

There is no human situation or dimension completely devoid of conflict; the religious dimension, among others, is always concretely involved in historic tensions because of the ideological representations it conveys. That is why every call to the celebration of forgiveness will be ambiguous and mystifying up to a certain point; moreover, it is not rare that it may give rise to anxiety and even anger. There is no hope of living an absolutely "pure" celebration of forgiveness.[4]

Celebrations of forgiveness are always lived in ambiguity; but so that they may not be too mystifying, "co-opting" the participants, some conditions are necessary to insure a minimum of authenticity. We have pointed out some of them: the recognition of conflicts and of the impossibility of concluding them too rapidly; the recognition of a certain fundamental inequality between partners, so that their dialogue will not be twisted; the acknowledgement that none of the parties can be considered entirely "just," but that, on the contrary, each has to ask forgiveness; the acknowlegement of the impossibility, especially for the powerful, to understand entirely the point of view of the "others"; the acknowledgement of a mutual need for forgiveness; the will to work as seriously and as effectively as possible for the establishment of a greater justice in the areas where there are conflicts; and, finally, the recognition of all the dimensions, with all their conscious and unconscious or non-intentional mechanisms. Without these conditions and the precise analyses that they demand, celebration of forgiveness could become a masquerade where some will finally be oppressed and exploited. And, when these conditions are present, it is important that, in a society, some voices are raised in the name of the "others" in order to call communities to celebrate forgiveness. It is this openness to "otherness" that gives a religious[5] — as distinguished from political — dimension to forgiveness. It also explains how Churches can become symbolic places for forgiveness, by conferring on it a public dimension.

An Example:
Christian Celebrations of Forgiveness

It is easy to show the ambiguities of varied notions of forgiveness, but it is not so easy to recommend a positive structure for a celebration of forgiveness. On what societal projects and ideologies are celebrations of forgiveness based and who receives privileges from them?[6] We will consider some traditional structures of Christian celebrations of forgiveness and examine how they reckon with the analyses we have presented.

Christian rites of forgiveness begin by reminding people of the reality of evil or sinfulness in our human history. The liturgical texts used in the beginning of Lent are typical in this regard. They call the community to listen to the cries of the oppressed, orphans, prisoners. Then prophetic voices remind us that God is not indifferent with respect to this evil. (Such an approach could also be experienced in groups of non-believers, but there the prophetic voices would not refer to a transcendent presence.) This confrontation with evil in history is the foundation of the Christian dynamic of forgiveness.

In our culture, it is difficult for people to recognize precisely their personal implication in evil, without individualizing the problem by a sterile or unhealthy guilt. The Catholic practice of confession has, at times, been disasterous in this regard. However, in the ritualized avowal, we can name evil and say how we participate in it without situating this "confession" in the context of an analytical calculation of rights and wrongs. This "confession" only makes sense in the background of a yearning for greater justice; unfortunately, this yearning is too often expressed in a notion of regret, which, for all practical purposes, serves to reduce the celebration to a moralizing process. However, when it is appropriately dealt with, "confession of sins" has an effect of naming evil and of opening up a future; it creates an entry point for moving beyond all the ways we use to isolate ourselves in the certainty (whether individual or collective) of being right.

But confession of sins can also be ambiguous because to acknowledge one's participation in evil can sometimes have the effect of weighing down certain groups or individuals who are already too vulnerable. For example, it can be detrimental for a group of South African blacks — already conditioned to undervalue themselves — to admit their participation in this precise evil which is racism. On the individual level, the same can happen when, for example, a partner recognizes his or her part in the hurts and sufferings in a marriage. Moreover, the confession of "sin" can easily enter into resonance with a scrupulous psychology which already has too little trust in self.

The next step in the Christian dynamics of forgiveness is its proclamation. The issue arises then to know *who* may proclaim forgiveness, that is, who can ritually say that we are accepted without making this proclamation a manipulation of the group? It is important that forgiveness be expressed by the party having been hurt, for example, by one of the partners in a marriage, but this is not always feasible, and it especially risks being intermingled in the slow negotiation of a reconciliation. Forgiveness "in the name of God" by someone speaking neither his or her name, nor the name of one of the parties, but from a communal commission, can be an appropriate symbolic procedure to signify openness, acceptance and a call to go "beyond conflicts." Unfortunately, this symbolic and ritual role of the priest has often been either guilt-inducing or an easy solution by which people avoid encountering those who have actually been hurt.

If it is not accompanied by a concrete commitment against evil, the proclamation that one is loved, in spite of the evil in which one participates, can conceal the reality of the conflicts that exist. It is probably for this reason that the Christian celebration of forgiveness returns toward "something to do" and makes reference to a symbolic action (a penance) destined to invite participants to concretely engage in the battle against evil.

Christian dynamics of forgiveness degenerate at times into sclerotic, if not perverse, rites. Forgiveness has to be renewed so as to allow individuals or groups to be confronted with evil in their history and to go beyond the conflictual dimension of their life without suppressing it. Such celebrations of forgiveness — whether they are a part of daily existence or whether they be special and privileged moments — are not primarily destined to resolve conflicts but, rather, to help people not to be enclosed in them and the measuring attitudes they convey. It is not rare that a celebration of forgiveness — lived with the conditions required for its authenticity — leads to a new way of seeing what is at stake in life; it then is often a step toward some partial reconciliation.

Finally, Measurement or Forgiveness?

If forgiveness and analysis are necessary, can we set a priority between these two attitudes? In the end, which is of prime importance — the logic of measuring shortcomings and calculating blame in conflicts (the logic of the scapegoat) or the dynamics of forgiveness? The effects of the language used in this regard depend upon the context of their social and interpersonal conditions. It can, however, be interesting to note once again the hope which pervades Christianity, a hope related to the proclamation of forgiveness of sins and of remission of debts. The Gospel seems to affirm that, ultimately, the measurement of faults leads to an impasse. It emphasizes that it is necessary that, if people wish to get out of this deadlock, they ultimately have to live conflicts without measuring the adverse parts and enclosing them in a logic of rights and wrongs. This, by no means, diminishes the importance of negotiating conflicts and engaging in struggles. It does, however, institute beyond these tensions and without denying them, another logic well described by the psalmist: "If you measure faults, who then will endure?"

DISCUSSION QUESTIONS

1. Why is it that the notion of forgiveness takes a different meaning when used in an interpersonal or in a collective context?

2. Why is it important to analyze situations? What are the differences between the weak and the powerful when the question of analysis rises?

3. What happens when everything is measured? What is the so-called "logic of the scapegoat"?

4. Analyze the concept of forgiveness as an openness beyond the world of measurement.

5. How central is forgiveness to the message of the Gospel?

6. Analyze the difference between forgiveness and reconciliation. Does forgiveness necessarily imply that the conflicts have come to an end?

7. Does asking for forgiveness imply that we were wrong?

8. Relate forgiving and forgetting.

9. What is the difficulty when the question of forgiveness comes for a collectivity?

10. Is is possible to build a complete "theory" of forgiveness? Why not?

11. What is the ambiguity of a call to forgiveness? Who can call to forgiveness?

12. Under which conditions can a celebration of forgiveness avoid being a manipulation and an oppression?

13. Investigate the meaning of the concept "confession of sins," beyond the calculation of rights and wrongs.

14. Give some conditions for a proclamation of forgiveness to be meaningful.

[1]One of the functions of the myth and Christian doctrine of "original sin," is to present evil historically, in such a way that it no longer makes sense to designate a contemporary scapegoat as the root of all evil. There is more on that subject in the work of René Girard.

[2]Forgiveness is not the only means of transgressing the logic of measurement; a "great burst of laughter," for example, can also do it, as well as a strategy of non-violence or a unilateral disarmament.

[3]There are, however, enough similarities between both situations to make use of the notion of forgiveness legitimately because the individual "subject" should not be taken for granted more than the collective "subject." To say "I" implies a kind of a forceful decision through which I dare to affirm myself beyond my ambiguous motivations or determinisms.

[4]Cf. G. Fourez: *Sacraments and Passages,* Ave Maria Press, 1983, in the appendix.

[5]We here understand religious traditions in their broadest sense, as a call in the name of some "ultimate reality" in history which transcends particular conflicts.

[6]This problem is more of a general one. A celebration is always a way of going beyond the limits of daily analysis; therefore, it transcends "political interactions" in a certain way. But the institution of a celebration (and all celebrations are institutionalized) is an essentially political act, because the celebration reinforces and assumes a particular social organization.

[7]This chapter has been written with the collaboration of J. Briard, M. Cheza, J. Somer and P. Tihom, members of the religious team of *La Revue Nouvelle* which signs *Placide.* It was published in this magazine in September, 1983.

21
GOD IS LOVE

Many Christians take for granted that they believe that God is love. They know that it is part of the Christian message, and they would be quite amazed if someone suggested that they do not believe so. But that is the case. To be convinced, we only have to see how people react when they think about God. While they say they believe God is love, they act as if God were frightening. For example, if a person thinking about God, considers first what he *should* do to please him, he does not react as one who believes that God is love. Even worse, when some people think about God, they fear God's judgment. Some people even spend their lives trying to avoid punishment. That is not the way people respond to those who love them. Thus, one should carefully distinguish between what people say they believe and what they do believe. One has to recognize that the God for many Christians is not a God of love, but a judging and condemning God, someone whom we should be careful not to displease, a frightening God.

To discover what our idea of God is, let us examine our reactions when thinking about God. If they are similar to those we have for the person whom we believe loves us the most, we may conclude that we believe God is love. If, on the contrary, we can find people with whom we feel more at ease than we do with God, we have to conclude that the God we believe in is not as good as we are or as people are. A story helps to explain the difference.

A friend lost his mother in a car accident. She had been divorced and was living with another man. He was upset because his mother had died, according to the catechism, in a state of sin. He therefore was concerned about her salvation. When he was asked if he felt his mother was a good person and if he would condemn her, he answered that she was a good and loving person and that *he* would never condemn her. The only logical conclusion from his anxious reaction is that he believed that God was not as beneficent as he was. And when people believe in a God who is less good than they are, then, as the French philosopher Prudhom said, they become atheists. Actually, it is quite good that they do so because if they believe in such a God they would certainly not believe in the loving God of Christians, but in an idol.

On the contrary, if we believe that God is love, we feel accepted before God and not threatened. If we believe that God is love, that means we think God loves us for our own sake and not for any other reason. At the same time, we also realize that God looks at us with hope. We are completely accepted, but God hopes that we will grow, be ourselves and bear fruit in abundance. To believe in a loving God means to believe we are accepted and known, without feeling any fear on our part. That is what St. John stresses in his Epistle: perfect love casts away fear.

When we are with somebody who loves us, we are not afraid even if we make mistakes. We know we are accepted, and love liberates us from all the fears caused by our limitations, our mistakes and even inmost selves. It is true that human love casts out fear; and, as St. John points out, we do not know that God is love if that love does not free us from our fears (1 Jn 4). It is the love of God which frees us in such a way that we need no longer be afraid of either life or death. And, even more, we are no longer afraid of people. If after all this, we discover that we still are frightened, it means we do not believe in a loving God. And actually, it seems we never completely believe in a loving God; all of us are still afraid in some way.

St. John goes even further when he says that if we believe in the love of God, there will be no fear of punishment. When we are afraid of punishment, we do not understand that Jesus came for sinners, not for the just. He came to save, not to condemn. This part of the Good News is obvious when we believe in a loving God. But it seems as if many Christians do not believe in such a God. The meaning of the Good News is veiled to those who cannot understand how great God's love is and who prefer to build an image of God similar to themselves.

To say that God is love means then that God loves us for ourselves and wants us to exist as a uniquely other person. To love someone is to want that person to be able to exist in his or her own right and even to be able to build a life in a very different way than we would imagine it for ourselves. God would be a poor lover if the beloved had to be a slavish imitation of the lover. For that reason, believing that God has a blueprint for our lives contradicts that doctrine that God is love. True love does not create such dependency; it wants the beloved to be free and able to create his or her own life. We should be prudent, therefore, when saying that we depend on God. If we mean we depend on God in the same way that a beloved finds strength, freedom and independence in the other's love, then we share that relationship with God. But if to depend on God means that we are unable to function independently, as a child cannot function without its mother, it would be inappropriate to say that there is such a relationship with God.

The love of God makes us free, creative, and independent, exactly as true human love does. The French poet, Peguy, has expressed that quite well when he pictures God looking at humanity before going to sleep and thinking, "What amazes me each time I look at human beings is that I created them free. And then I do not know what will be the new thing they will discover tomorrow, which will amaze me." Such an idea is just the opposite of a vocation perceived as a blueprint for our life. But it is much more appropriate. God loves us enough to want our lives to be ours and not a product of the divine imagination.

This love is unconditional and without any strings attached to it. This can be understood again in comparing it with human love. If a so-called friend says to us, "I will love you if you do such and such a trying; but if you do not, you will lose my friendship," we know that there is not much to lose of that friendship because it is not true love. Unfortunately, too many Christians seem to believe that God loves them in such a way. But, according to the Good News, the love of God is unconditional and that is why it can cast out fear in those who believe. This unconditional love does not mean a lack of care about what we do, which would be in effect a lack of love. It does mean that in whatever we decide to do, we are accepted as we are, with our decisions. God looks at us with love and hope, asking what we want to do with our lives as we experience this love, desiring our growth to full human maturity and staying with us through all of life.

When we love someone, we want that person to be happy. So it is with God who also desires our happiness. Jesus came so that we would have joy and that our joy would be perfect, as John says. He also said that Jesus wants us to have life abundantly. That has a simple and obvious consequence. If we believe that, because of God, we should be less happy, we are mistaken. God does not ask us to be a slave or a drudge. On the contrary, God wants all of humanity to be fulfilled; and that is the only meaning of the will of God.

Finally, it is important to stress that God does not love us because we are good persons but, quoting again St. John: "God loves us when we were still sinners." Jesus did not come to judge or to condemn but to save and to liberate. Whatever sins we would like to have forgiven are not an impediment in our encounter with him. The simple story of the adulterous woman illustrates this. The woman had committed a gross sin: according to the law and human teaching she had to be punished by being stoned. But Jesus refused to argue. He confronted the

Jews with the love of God and their own need to be loved and to be forgiven. They, therefore, did not dare to condemn her. And Jesus also refused to condemn her. He let her go, hoping that she would grow in love. That does not mean that she would necessarily stop sinning, but that the love of God is greater than all the human ideas about it. When Christians realize that the love of God is so great, they believe in the Good News, God loves us.[1]

DISCUSSION QUESTIONS

1. Show the difference between believing that God is love in theory, and in reality.

2. Comment on the statement of John: "Perfect love casts away fear," and apply it to the belief that God is love.

3. Analyze the concept of being dependent on God in relationship with the beliefs that God is love.

4. Relate the concept of "justification by faith" and the belief in God's love.

---

[1]In this chapter, I emphasized an interpersonal and psychological model to speak of God's love. This model could be completed by speaking of God's love in societal structures. The Gospels as well as the Epistles of Paul (cf. Philippians 2:6-11) also describe God's love as a solidarity with the poor, the oppressed, those in an enslaved condition. To complete an image of a loving God, God has to be recognized not only as relating to individuals, but also as being in solidarity with those groups that suffer and are crushed in historical social structures.

22
PRAYER AND CELEBRATION IN THE CHRISTIAN COMMUNITY

The question of prayer is a highly complex one, and it would be senseless to try to deal with it thoroughly in only a few pages. For this reason, definite answers will not be proposed here. The point of view developed below will certainly not exhaust Christian tradition; it will emphasize an aspect of prayer which could possibly respond to a need of a society too often deprived of celebration.

Concerning the topic of Christian prayer, we would like to suggest a distinction between Prayer and prayer. The former may be considered as the profound attitude of heart of the Christian in the presence of God. But, according to the particular psychological makeup of the person, this attitude will be expressed in many ways, for example, openness, acceptance, intimacy, silence. Thus the term prayer will be used to designate those particular behaviors through which the Christian tries to foster Prayer. Obviously, Prayer and prayer cannot be separated. There will be no Prayer unless it is, in one way or another, expressed in a concrete response springing from the psychological make-up of the Christian. Consequently, it is impossible to treat the one without treating the other. This essay will set out to consider the topic of prayer. It will be within this consideration that the subject of Prayer will be touched upon.

Prayer belongs to the realm of a human relationship with God. That is why the notion of *relationship* itself becomes highly relevant to this subject. Human relationships seem always to include two factors, interaction between persons and celebration of the relationshp itself. If a relationship consists only in deeds, and the parties never stop to celebrate what is happening, those actions will soon lose their meaning and become merely tasks. They will no longer be a way of encountering persons. On the other hand, if there were only *celebration* of the relationship, that would eventually become a celebration of nothing. The celebration would soon become empty. So our relationship to God will include these two aspects of any interpersonal relationship — deeds and celebration. On this basis, we now suggest that prayer is essentially the celebration of our relationship with the Transcendent whom we call God.

A celebration will usually contain at least two elements, intellectual and ritual. Some intellectual understanding of what is being celebrated must be presented, but there is also need for a gesture, a word, a silence — a sign, which indicates that what is being celebrated goes far beyond what can be rationally comprehended. In marriage, for example, the sex act can become the bearer of what is ineffable in the relationship. Some kind of "ritual" gesture is probably necessary. So prayer too will have these aspects of relationship; the intellectual (often called "meditation") and the ritual (gestures, words, silences). Obviously, these elements will take varied forms depending on personality or on environment and culture.

We do not pray to make God aware of us, but to help us to retain an awareness of God's presence in our life. Thus, prayer is our human way of keeping ourselves aware that there is a transcendent meaning to our life[1] and that in every person there is a dimension deeper than all understanding. Every human action which helps us to keep aware of this can be called "prayer," even if we are not accustomed to call it by that name.[2] Just as an unconscious smile may be the symbol of love, our prayer need not always be explicit and conscious. But whether explicit or not, prayer will always be a celebration of awareness; as such, it should encompass all the dimensions and all the interactions of the person.

People are always involved in two types of interaction: first, that relationship to our own selves in our own interior aloneness; and second, those relationships in which our own selves are united with others. Consequently, the life of prayer will always have both an individual and a communal aspect.

Individual prayer may be thought of as that psychological event through which we become individually aware of, and more open to, the presence of God. Accepting prayer as a psychological event enables us to find our way out of the familiar prayer-dilemma: "While praying, do I really speak to God or only to myself?" It is this writer's opinion that such a dichotomy is false: the psychological event of speaking to oneself can be precisely the manifestation of God's presence within a human psychology. Thus we will not look to the psychological perception of the prayer itself to ascertain if it is "authentic" or "inauthentic." The only criteria traditionally accepted in both the gospel and the Church are the fruits of prayer. If prayer helps to promote the signs of the Kingdom in and around us (prisoners are freed, the afflicted are consoled, etc.). then our prayer manifests its authenticity. If, on the contrary, these signs do not appear (especially if prayer is producing fear in place of love and responsible freedom), then that prayer is not a manifestation of God's presence among us — despite any good or "holy" feelings it might have produced.

If prayer is a psychological event, we can readily see that there will be as many different "types" of prayer as there are individuals, each with a unique psychological make-up. For the purposes of this essay, however, we will broadly classify prayer into four important theological types: Christocentric prayer, Spirit-centered prayer, Father-centered prayer and "non-religious" prayer. In no way is this classification exhaustive, and, indeed, it is based on stereotypes. No real person can fit into any type and almost every Christian includes some of the four types in their prayer, although in varying degrees. The classification, however, can help to indicate the thrust of the prayer life of different individuals.

Christocentric prayer, for example, is characterized by the important part played by the person of Jesus. Persons drawn to this type of prayer will construct a psychological image of Jesus. They speak to him as they would to a friend. This implies that they project a great deal of feeling and emotion into their imagination. If their prayer is authentic, these psychological feelings will bring forth the signs of the Kingdom. Consequently, they will bear witness that this prayer is truly an epiphany of God. On the other hand, if this prayer leads to withdrawal into one's feelings and imagination, Christian tradition usually calls it "illusion." This does not mean that the projected image of Jesus in the authentic prayer is a different psychological event from that met in the illusory prayer. The difference between illusion and authentic prayer is discerned not by the psychological content of the prayer, but by its fruits. Prayer which bears good fruit is "real" prayer and that which bears none is only emptiness.

For others the experience of prayer is different. Instead of "speaking" to God or to Jesus, they emphasize being open to the working of the Spirit in their lives. Their prayer is centered on the presence of the Spirit in the actual moment. In prayer they try to open themselves to the action of this Spirit and to the growth he is inspiring in others. The above-mentioned criteria hold here also; if the fruits of the Kingdom are present, if the liberation for which all creation is yearning is manifested, the prayer can be evaluated as authentic. But, if instead of liberation, there is domination of others, enslavement and wounding of persons, then God is not present.

At the present time there is an increasing development of this Spirit-centered type of inner life. It is especially common among those with higher education and those who feel that the coming of the Kingdom is experienced in continuous growth and liberation.

Another spirituality finds its focus in the Father. The prayer of the Christian who tends to see God as "Father" is usually simple and silent. It tends to be the acceptance of the gift of the Father: the gift of life, of one's own being, of gratuitous love and joy. This prayerful celebration of the relationship to the Father will consist mainly in *being* and in joyfully accepting being. The fruits of this prayer are a tremendous freedom and boldness in accomplishing all that such a person feels called to do. In deep peace, such persons are certain that they are beloved of the Father, so that there is no room for fear or forgiveness. They are aware of being sent by the Father and they accept that mission peacefully. As a fruit of that prayer, life is seen not as a drudgery, but as a great thing which is happening. If prayer directed to the Father produces these signs, there is good reason to believe that God is present. Confronted with these psychological feelings, many will ask the above-mentioned question: "Am I really speaking to God when praying or only speaking to myself?"

Our point of view allows the following answer. We are speaking to a psychologically constructed and projected image of God; but, if that psychological event opens our eyes to the Transcendent, then we are really communicating with God. In other words, speaking to "oneself" (that is, to the constructed image of God) and speaking to God are not mutually exclusive events. However it is useful to compare the image of Jesus that one has constructed with the one described in the Gospel. That contemplation of Jesus in the Gospel saves us from narrowing God to our own dimensions.

We will characterize our final category of prayer as "non-religious."[3] Many people today seem to experience the Transcendent in non-religious patterns. They celebrate life and all that it holds, without any specific reference to religious concepts. "Religious" terminology is not relevant for them and they express what transpires in the depths of their being in other terms. They may use the word "God," but often even that term is abandoned. Usually, they turn to psychology for the vocabulary in which to express their experience, e.g., they will talk about "dropping one's defenses" with respect to God (or, perhaps, to "life"). In many cases they are touched by the message of the gospel, but they do not express their experience in religious categories. They are struck by that person, Jesus, who seems to manifest to them what life is all about.

Christians would benefit by seeing this approach as basically healthy, even if they sometimes feel threatened by it. It is a reminder of the traditional doctrine which states that we do not meet Jesus through an understanding of God, but that we understand God through meeting Jesus. In other words, we do not understand who Jesus is by means of our religious concept of God, but we begin to understand what life is all about (and consequently, who God is) through Jesus Christ. That is why, even for those who explicitly call themselves "Christians," there are times when "religious" concepts appear inadequate or irrelevant. It happens also because of the way religious vocabulary has been abused. At these moments it is important to recognize the value of the "non-religious" prayers. In religious terms we would say that they are inspired by the Spirit and genuinely Christian. Here also, as before, it is by means of the criteria of its fruits that the value of the prayer will be discerned.

All of these spiritualities are quite different, and we must accept this difference, even if some individuals will feel uneasy in the presence of a prayer which is not their own. Unfortunately, it is not rare to find people "anathematizing" others because they pray differently. This can happen in more than one way. For example the sophisticate will despise the prayer of the simple or the simple person will find it hard to understand why popular symbols do not mean very much to some "intellectuals." Since the sophisticate usually has more means of defense for positions taken, let us especially stress the danger of looking down on — or even disregarding — "old" and simple ways of praying.

Some people will get very upset when they discover that prayer is a "psychological event." When they perceive that their image of Jesus is a psychological projection, they falsely conclude that their prayer must be unauthentic. What is forgotten here is that any prayer is psychologically constructed.[4] Here again, it is the manifestation of the fruits of the Kingdom which is the only criterion. Perhaps some of these "upset" people are yielding to the gnostic temptation of believing that the less our human psyche is involved, the better the prayer. Besides revealing a great naiveté of human psychology and especially the role of the unconscious, such a point of view often leads to denying others the liberty to be themselves in their authentic expression of prayer. The rosary, for example, despite what such purists may think, can be an authentic prayer producing deeply Christian and liberating love. It has even produced some authentic Christian revolutionaries.

In the above discussion we have investigated different spiritualities through the use of theological categories. But psychological categories can also be very useful. Let us, for example, use Jung's classification. He distinguishes among the "feelers," the "intuitives," the "thinkers," and the "pragmatists" (or "sensates"). With reference to these types we can distinguish, accordingly, different types of prayer. The "feeler" will find silent prayer very appealing, while the "intuitive" will be drawn to contemplate; the "thinker" will like to meditate and, finally, the "pragmatist" will want to do something, like lighting a candle or even feeling the beads. And all these people are necessary for the fullest celebration of all the gifts of God.

As we have just suggested in these differences — and, indeed, through them — we receive a call to growth. The differences remind us that no one can have the "last word" as far as God is concerned and that no prayer can be "complete." The experience of meeting someone who prays differently leads to the awareness[5] of the fact that our view is limited and imperfect. We then experience existentially that we are not God! Such an experience can be quite an occasion for growth.

Dostoyevsky in *The Brothers Karamazov* describes such a situation. A young man, an anarchist and an unbeliever, was dying. "His old nurse would come in and say, 'let me light the lamp before the Icon, dear.' Previously, the young man would not let her do it and he even used to blow it out. But now he would say: 'Light it, my dear. I was a beast not to let you before. You pray to God when lighting the lamp and I am praying when I rejoice in looking at you. So we are praying to one and the same God.'"

This text, which needs no comment, shows how the acknowledgement of the validity of someone else's prayer can open the way to a deeper encounter with the God who is beyond all our limited views.

To give value to a form of prayer which is not our own does not in any way mean that we should limit ourselves to a superstitious way of praying. This would prevent us from being really open to the Spirit in our own life. As always, we can only look to the effect brought in our life when seeking to ascertain our way of prayer. It is to be remembered, however, that, as with all human actions, every prayer life will suffer from a certain amount of ambivalence. This ambivalence does not have to be resolved on the spot. That is the meaning of the parable of the field where the good wheat and the weeds were allowed to grow together (Mt 13).

We have stressed that prayer is a celebration leading to a growing awareness of God's presence in our lives. It will be expressed in various ways according to individual psychologies, educational backgrounds and cultural heritages. To realize that there are different ways of praying — and that they are all limited — is, perhaps, an essential aspect of the experience of God. But any celebration, any awareness, would be unfulfilled if it were only an individual experience. That is why there must be communal prayer, that is, a communal celebration culminating in a communal awareness of God's presence among us. Just as with individual prayer, this prayer will contain both intellectual and ritual elements.

In the past, it was easy to attain a group experience of the presence of God within a community. The culture of agrarian societies was relatively stable and people within a given community had much in common, sharing a common background. Even though there was a certain amount of diversity (which was expressed by different spiritualities), that diversity was hardly noticeable in the praying community. The prayer experience of the group was the result of the common acculturation; the traditions of communal prayer had been passed on within the group. In communities of religious the novitiate usually provided the unity of religious culture necessary for communal prayer.

Today, in contrast, it seems that achieving a unity of experience is more difficult, if not impossible. As the roles individuals play in society have become more diverse, as education has become more specialized, it seems that the hope of an easy unity has vanished. There is, however, an alternative which has proved quite successful — communal sharing. If unity of thought can be longer be taken for granted, it is possible to *share* the *diversity* of our experiences of God. It would seem that this sharing must be an essential part of the life of any community which wants to live today as a praying community. In the presence of real differences of background, any prayer celebration would be empty without some knowledge of what the others think and value. This is why, at present, there is within the Christian community a movement toward more sharing. It is not a passing fashion, but a valid response to a real need.

With the acceptance of this increased diversity, ritual celebration takes on a new importance. Today it is obvious that any semantic agreement on what the "experience of God" means would be false and only mask very different outlooks. Consequently, we must introduce gestures, nonintellectual cultic acts, which will give expression to the fact that we profess to be one in God despite all diversity.

Remembering the categories of personalities proposed by Jung, we can see that a good communal celebration will try to provide a variety of symbols so that each type person can find

something to which to relate: there must be silence for the
"feelers," some vision for the "intuitives," something to understand for the "thinkers," and something to *do* for the "pragmatists." Since in prayer the whole life of individuals and of
communities is symbolized, it will take diverse forms according
to placeds, social classes, specific conflicts and historical situations. Prayer is not the same when a community celebrates
some achievement and when a member of a guerrilla group
has been captured, tortured and killed.

The eucharistic celebration can sum up all the necessary
elements of communal prayer. At the psychological level a good
liturgy provides for each personality type. Considering it on a
deeper level we can see its structure as providing an opportunity
for celebrating what Christian life is all about. The liturgy of
reconciliation, at the beginning of the celebration, manifests
unity in the tensions of diversity. The liturgy of the word allows
for the sharing of insights. In the eucharistic prayer we have
the elements of ritual. These rituals are never understood completely. At this moment the faithful are confronted with the
heart of the Christian mystery: Jesus laying down his life for
those he loves.

Prayer has been presented as the celebration of God's presence. It fulfills the human need to go beyond function and
task. In prayer, men and women celebrate the awareness of
who they are and what is the totality of all the dimensions of
their life. Such a celebration, distinct from the needs of everyday
life, will include both intellectual and ritual elements. These
will vary according to the cultural and psychological background of each person. Insofar as it is the celebration of a
relationship, prayer will have both an individual and a communal aspect. At the individual level it is a part of that "inner
life" which is necessary to every person. Communally, it is
manifested in a shared understanding and a participation in
a ritual expressive of the ineffable. In essence, the eucharist is
a paradigm of all Christian celebration.

DISCUSSION QUESTIONS

1. What distinction is made in this chapter between Prayer and prayer?

2. How can prayer be defined as a celebration of life?

3. Do we pray becaue of God or because of our human psychology? In what sense can both answers be meaningful?

4. How does this chapter deal with dilemma: "When I pray, do I speak to God, or is prayer an event in my psychology?"

5. Give different ways in which a prayer can be centered. Explain what could be a Christocentric prayer, a prayer centered on the Spirit, a prayer focused on the Father.

6. Explain the notion of "non-religious prayer."

7. Why does prayer life need both an individual and a communal dimension?

8. How does the diversity of spiritualities speak of transcendent God?

9. Why is, in our contemporary world, "sharing" essential to a prayer life?

10. How will prayer be different for feelers, thinkers, pragmatists and intuitive people? How is it possible to provide celebrations that will feed the need of all these different types of people?

11. Is it fair to equate prayer life to "inner life"?

---

[1]It might be of interest to note here the ambiguity of the term "inner life." Ity can be used both in a psychological and a religious sense. It is natural for people to reflect upon their life as they grow in awareness. People use the term "inner life" to indicate this growing awareness of reality and the ability to reflect upon it. To have an "inner life" is considered necessary for psychological health. Now, we suggest, if a person's life has a transcendent dimension, it will enter into his or her inner life; this is prayer.

[2]In more philosophical terms, prayer might be called any action which symbolizes our relationship with God. A symbol could be understood as the concurrence of understanding and gesture resulting in a new awareness.

[3]We use the term in the sense Dietrich Bonhoeffer did.

[4]It can even happen that authentic prayer is neurotically constructed.

[5]This is more than an intellectual conviction.

23
THE CONTEMPLATIVE LIFE
IN AN EFFICIENT WORLD[1]

Today a number of people consider the contemplative life useless and irrelevant. They believe that monasteries (Christian, Buddhist and others) are meaningless since they contribute neither to the building of the modern world nor to the struggle for liberation. They claim that contemplatives live irresponsible lives apart from the problems of our big cities and the tensions of our scientific world.

This chapter will address itself to evaluating this claim of irresponsibility and will propose a hypothesis according to which contemplative life is not only relevant to our modern civilization, but essential for its survival. Obviously, this does not mean that we imagine that contemplative life as it is lived today is always an adequate expression of the contemplative ideal. It is quite possible that many monasteries fail in their unique mission while some lay persons — Christian or not Christian — can live a contemplative lifestyle.

In this essay, I will not elaborate a complete theory of contemplative life; rather I will attempt to understand the meaning of the contemplative lifestyle in relation to our present culture without reference to its complete religious meaning. I will, therefore, examine only the social implications of the contemplative life. In doing this I choose to speak solely about the human meaning of the contemplative life insofar as it is significant for society. This is a limited consideration, yet it goes to the heart of the matter, for an essential aspect of the contemplative lifestyle is to be a *sign* for Christians and for the entire human community. As Thomas Aquinas has said, we do not pray for the sake of God, but because we are human beings, which is to say that prayer is a personal and social *sign* of some dimension of human life.

In what follows, I will present some aspects of modern society and show how contemplative life is a meaningful challenge to our culture. To put it briefly, my hypothesis will be that our culture is dominated by the efficiency principle, while a contemplative lifestyle challenges that principle by going beyond it.

It has been said again and again that the base of our culture is efficiency. Herbert Marcuse has analyzed this phenomenon in *Eros and Civilization* and *The One Dimensional Man.* He has shown that our contemporaries give tremendous and unique importance to efficiency in accomplishing a task. They commit themselves to build a civilization, and, in view of that, agree to repress their spontaneity. People seem to be enclosing themselves in a limited culture taken as an ultimate end. Not only have they agreed, as is necessary, to limit their spontaneity and their freedom by reality; they even feel guilty whenever they are not doing what they are expected to do and when they are simply enjoying life. In this culture, pure spontaneity, the joy of being, simply for the sake of being, is often considered strange if not bad. People seem to have created for themselves a completely task-oriented universe; even religious have accepted this standard of efficiency. Was it not often believed that, to be good religious, people had to repress their spontaneity, to be "perfect"? A religious could not meet people unless he or she had some business to deal with them. A purely social relationship would have been considered idle. All had to be oriented to only one goal: the efficient building of the Kingdom, with an efficiency principle even applied to individual holiness. When the world is conceived in such a manner, nothing is gratuitous anymore. People have gone so far as to calculate the relative merits of a way of life. In that respect, contemplative life has been very much assimilated by our civilization of efficiency. It has too often allowed itself to be evaluated according to that principle.

Our culture is hungry for people who would be people-oriented and would refuse to have their spontaneity suppressed by the efficiency principle. Our culture is hungry to find people who feel that it is enough to be a person, enough to be simply defined by their relationship to God and to others. I believe that this is the characteristic of the "contemplative." Contemplatives do not want to be defined by their job, by the results of their work, but simply by their relationships, by their being. Such a way of life is a deviation from the patterns of our society, but a quite meaningful deviation. It reminds us that we do not have to be defined by what we do but by what we are. Could we not say that the contemplative is a person for whom it is enough to live, to be loved and to love. Such persons would certainly work, because it is necessary to work to live, but they would not have their work guided by the principle of efficiency (even if their work must be efficient!). Their work would rather be a way of being with people and with God. In all things they would simply enjoy the wonders which are coming from love; they would have really chosen the best part. And this life, even if it would not be lived under the *principle of efficiency* would be completely *meaningful* (and sometimes quite *efficient*) because it would help people to realize that *they* also do not have to be defined by what they do. For them also, it is enough to be.

In fact, by simply being, contemplatives created space in which others can also *be* and *be freely.* They are like those older persons who have succeeded — while getting old — in enjoying life, hope and love; they are making everybody happy around them. In fact, the contemplative is anticipating the time of old age when every person has to become a contemplative; older persons, if they wish to be happy, have to define themselves simply by what they are and not by what they do. Contemplative religious, in a prophetic and meaningful way, anticipate that moment of life.

To enjoy life as a contemplative is not an easy thing; there is a difficult balance to be found between an easy-going life and a task-oriented one. The danger of refusing the existence of *reality* and *work* is real. Contemplative life could also be a way of evading the confrontation with evil in society and in history, of promoting an ideology which conceals social struggles and of escaping the necessary choices of solidarity. But, as we have already seen, the danger is as great in the other direction: the danger of making of contemplative life a new *task*. It is not easy to accept the principle of reality in the contemplative life without beginning to make of this life a job again. To do so, the principle of reality should not be introduced by an abstract law, but by living persons. The persons who choose to live that gratuitous life will always be challenged by the encounter with the Other and the others; as long as they will accept deeply that God is God and that other people are really other, and that they are loved by them, it can be hoped that they will be able to enjoy both love and gratuitousness without getting into a selfish routine. To be confronted with reality, the contemplative has to be confronted with the Other and others. Contemplative life, then, does not have to prevent people from facing human history with its conflicts and contradictions.

Such life can be deeply fulfilling. However, it should be remembered that fulfillment is neither self-centered nor a reduction to one's self. Rather, each of us could say: "To be me, to be spontaneous, I do not want the Universe to be reduced to *my* dimension, but want the Universe *to be*, and then I will discover that I am me!" In that attitude, all the tradition of asceticism in contemplative life is included.

What could be the image of such a contemplative person? It can be characterized by a deep openness to all, in joy and respect, without trying to reduce others to his or her categories. Contemplatives will enjoy being themselves and permitting others to be themselves. They will be themselves in accepting love and loving in response, but that love will not be too possessive nor too aggressive, nor will they let themselves be possessed by the others. They will have a universal brotherly or sisterly love for all persons they meet, hoping in each meeting to grow into a new friendship. However, even if their lives are not centered around particular projects to free or to changte society, contemplatives have to choose their solidarities and to take sides in human struggles (if they pretend not to choose they effectively opt to be part of the conservative "silent majority"). It could even occur that the urgency of some action or the suffering of the oppressed may lead them to sacrifice their mystical protest to carry out some action among the struggles for human liberation. If they are Christian, they will be continually open to the Spirit of love and of liberation whom Jesus Christ has revealed to us.

Does such a pattern of life correspond to what contemplative life has traditionally been in the Catholic Church? In many details it seems not, the main difference being the emphasis on encountering God not only in oneself but also in others. Another difference refers to the way that I presented the separation from the world — what matters most in that respect is perhaps to confront evil and to protest against an unjust society, in the name of the Good News. To be separated from the world would then primarily mean to maintain a distance with respect to the dominant values of a society that has given priority to efficiency. But is this modern concept of contemplative life and separation from the world as different from traditional concepts as it might first appear? After all, the early Benedictine monasteries were not much more withdrawn from the world than the neighboring farms! In any case, by going beyond the efficiency principle, the tradition of contemplative life, renewed everyday, can continue to contribute greatly to the growth of our civilization!

DISCUSSION QUESTIONS
1. Analyze why in our contemporary society contemplative life seems to be a scandal.

2. Explain what Marcuse means by his efficiency (or performance) principle.

3. How does this chapter characterize a contemplative life style?

4. Criticize the statement: "Contemplatives work towards their perfection by praying all the time."

5. Does "to be a contemplative" mean to be beyond all human conflicts without choosing one's solidarities?

6. What is the specific gift of contemplative life in a society centered on efficiency?

7. Relate contemplative life and justification by faith.

[1]Part of this chapter was published in *The Catholic World*, January, 1971.

Epilogue
THE THREE
METAMORPHOSES OF THE
SPIRIT

At the beginning of this book I placed a quotation from Nietzsche on the three metamorphoses of the spirit. It might seem strange that a book explaining Christian faith would have an exergue taken from such an anti-Christian philosopher. However, there is only an apparent paradox, it seems to me. In this epilogue I would like to show that Christian faith is akin to this deep Nietzschean insight.

For Nietzsche, the spirit has three metamorphoses. First it is a camel, an animal accustomed to walk through the desert and to carry heavy loads. The camel is able to work and to travel a long way without stopping, as it submits to the order of its masters. Human beings do the same. They carry the heavy load of what is requested of them according to the norms of ethics, religion, reason or even science. When they live like camels, human beings can perform the most wonderful deeds, but they remain camels because they always feel they have to pattern their action according to an outside norm. Every ideal, even the idea of freedom, thus loads the spirit and enslaves people because ideals always serve to legitimate some established order (or disorder). The most sublime deeds performed in this phase of the spirit remain the work of the camel.

Then, says Nietzsche, the camel became a lion. A lion is a

217

rebel who breaks the bonds of the camel by fighting against the dragon; and the name of the dragon is: "You ought." Similarly human beings rebel against the weight which people and institutions impose upon them. They struggle to become free. But the lion is still unable to be free and to create because its energies are consumed in reaction against obligations imposed from without. And when the lion legitimizes a personal rebellion in the name of the ideal of freedom, it is not much different from the camel.

Then the lion becomes a child. The child does not justify what he or she does. He simply is; he plays. She can create, without wanting any justification. For Nietzsche, the child is no longer submissive, but simply affirms the self. The camel has to submit; the lion needs to rebel; the child just wants. It is not easy for human beings to come to the point when they stop justifying their action by saying that they need or have to act in some way; it is not easy to say: "That is what I want." Many prefer to abdicate their will and to resort to legitimations such as, "I have to," "I need to," etc. They never dare to say: "I myself want" or "I am somebody who has wishes, interests and drives." For Nietzsche, the child is not *better* than the camel or the lion (that would be a "camel-like" way of reasoning) but it so happens that the camel becomes a lion, and the lion a child. One cannot even say that a human being is *called* to say or is *allowed* to say "I want," because that would again be a way of legitimating one's will.

I believe that the Good News is related to these metamorphoses. People who rely on justification by works are like camels, and a liberation or a faith experience is what makes camels become children (by becoming first lions). In this way, the meaning of the traditional emphasis on the non-rationality of faith becomes clear. If faith were the result of a legitimating process, it could only produce camels. Faith and liberation are non-rational experiences through which human beings are freed to say: "I do not need legitimations any more"; I can say "I want." And at the same time the Christian concept of creation is hereby clarified. God does not want camels, he wants people who can respond as equals. And God cannot and does not want to force anybody to be so. God loves people and this love can liberate them. That is why there is meaning in saying also in this context that someone who does not become a child does not belong to the kingdom of God.

DISCUSSION QUESTIONS

1. Explain the metamorphoses of the spirit according to Nietzsche.
2. Relate these Nietzschean categories to the passage from justification by works to justification by faith.
3. What is the difference between the "camel's" image of God, and the "child's" image of God?

Appendix

At this point I wish to take up a few terms fairly common in Christian literature and comment briefly on each of them in the perspective of this essay.

CHURCH

The Church is not first of all an organization but the community of the faithful, the community of those who have been touched by their liberation in Christ and who, when living this liberation, can be signs of liberty for all people. If Christians really live, in words and deeds, this liberation, it will follow that they are rejected and persecuted as Christ was. (Cf. Part I, chapter 5.)

CONFLICT

Conflict is an essential element of Christian life, not because people like to be opposed, but because the affirmation of the Good News leads to conflicts. A conflict is an epiphany which reveals God in whom I discover the limit of my own message and I am able to open myself to the message of others. It is important for the Christian to love one's enemies. This implies that both the presence of enemies and the underlying conflict are acknowledged and also that beyond the conflictual aspect one knows how to love persons while continuing to struggle

with them. Conflicts also reveal the particularity of my culture
and of my class position. (Cf. Part III, chapter 19.)

CONVERSION

Christian conversion is the process (personal, cultural, political and economic) through which we discover that we are liberated by the love Jesus offers to us and which allows us to
live in a deeper liberty, beyond our old bondage. It brings a
change of spirit and of mentality as a result of which we do
not attempt to impose ourselves (or our faith) on others but
rather simply discover that we are accepted and freed and so
act accordingly. Conversion does not as much mean joining an
organization as being in communion with all those who proclaim
that the love of God has been revealed to them in Jesus and
who want to participate in God's own struggle against evil in
human society. (Cf. Part I, chapters 2 and 4.)

CREATION

Defining a created free person is a central question for Christians. For some, being a created person means that we are so
dependent on the Creator that we have to ask for permission
each time we make a decision (permission from God, from the
law, from moral codes, from reason, from science). The corres-
ponding image of God is the image of a dominating person. I
believe, on the contrary, that to be created by love is to be
established as a person who does not have to ask permission
to exist as a unique person. To believe in a loving Creator is
thus to have moved out of what Nietzsche calls the camel stage
and to be able to say "I want," without having to justify any
decision. That situation can only happen by "faith" because if
a permission or a reason is necessary for being able to say "I
want," one would be back to the "legitimating" attitude. This

is not to believe that God truly created free people. Consequently, to trust the creative love of God means to come to the discovery of one's own freedom and uniqueness, beyond all rational justification. (Cf. Part I, chapter 2 and Part III, chapter 21.)

DOMINANT GROUP

A group is said to be dominant if it imposes its law and order on the whole society. (Cf. Part I, chapter 7 and Part III, chapter 15.)

ETHICS AND FAITH

Christian faith is not a system of ethics. The mandate entrusted to us by Jesus cannot be the object of a commandment in the positivist sense of the term; Jesus' mandate is to love. Thus there is no Christian ethics if one interprets that to mean a series of commandments given particularly to Christians. However, it is also clear that the call of Christ implies well determined choices. Jesus always sides with the poor and oppressed, and against those who oppress them. (Cf. Part III, chapter 17.)

ESCHATOLOGY

Through this term the Christian tradition refers to the ultimate coming of Jesus Christ and the total establishment of the reign of God in opposition to the present historical dimension of life. When Christians refer to any part of their faith, both the eschatological (that is, the definitive) and the historical aspect have to be emphasized. For example, eschatologically the eucharist is the celebration of the complete gift of God, already present in some way today; but historically it is just the celebration of a limited and sinful community, hoping for an eschatological fulfillment which has not yet been realized. (Cf. Part I, chapter 5 and Part II, chapter 9.)

GOD

God is not to be separated from human existence and from the meeting of human beings. As St. John says in his Epistle, "No one has ever seen God." The Greek rendition is that there is no theory (or contemplation) of God outside of human experience. But as long as we love one another, God will live in us and the love of God will be complete in us" (John 4:12), or again, "We know that we have passed out of death and into life because we love our brothers" (John 3:14). The Christian affirms that it is in Jesus that we meet and know God. (Cf. Part I, chapter 6 and Part III, chapter 21.)

IDEOLOGICAL DOMINATION

When an ideology leads a particular group of people to have an image of itself such that this image supports the oppression of this group, that effect is described as ideological domination. Theologies can often be part of ideological domination. (Cf. Part I, chapter 2 and Part III, chapter 15.)

IDEOLOGY

In a broad sense, an ideology is any system of statements able to legitimate the action of a group or a subgroup. In a narrower sense, an ideology is a legitimating system which does not reveal whose class interest and privileges it defends.

It does not say who speaks in behalf of or against whom or what criteria underlie its statements. (Cf. Part I, chapter 6 and Part III, chapter 15.)

INCARNATION

The concept of incarnation can be seen in two different ways. The first is a more or less metaphysical concept by which one thinks first of God existing prior to incarnation and then appearing in his Son Jesus. Another point of view relies upon the affirmation that God is incarnated; it is in a human person that one finally meets God. This perspective takes the concrete aspect of the experience into account. It does not try to speculate what God would be if God were not revealed in humanity, especially in Jesus, "the image of the unseen God." (Cf. Part I, chapters 1 and 6.)

KINGDOM OF GOD

This is what is proclaimed by Jesus: the possibility of a way of life which surpasses the present reality in which people are locked in loveless opposition to one another. The Kingdom or reign of God is a way of life in which people discover that they are accepted through the gracious love of God or others (grace), and thus can accept each other in forgiveness and tenderness. (Cf. Part I, chapter 3.)

LITURGY AND PRAYER

These words characterize the celebration of God among us. We pray and we celebrate liturgies to symbolize — in the depths of our psyches and in our community — the action and the presence of God in our life. In particular, when Christians contemplate the Gospel and the life of Jesus Christ, they free themselves from a too narrow view of God which is only the projection of their own psychologies. (Cf. Part II, chapter 22; Part I, chapter 5; and Part II, chapters 9, 12 and 13.)

OPPRESSIVE RELATIONSHIP

A relationship is said to be oppressive if one of the parties has to submit to the other because if he/she would not, he/she would lose some security in life. (Cf. Part I, chapter 7.)

OUTSIDE THE CHURCH, NO SALVATION

This traditional formula is not to be interpreted as ordering people to enter first a group to be saved (or liberated). It means that there is no liberation in isolation and that consequently when there is no liberating community, there is no liberation, or at least, the liberation remains incomplete. Similarly, a purely individualistic liberation or a purely spiritual salvation, without a social and collective dimension, is declared meaningless by this affirmation. (Cf. Part I, chapters 3 and 4.)

SACRIFICE

The notion of sacrifice in reference to Jesus is extremely ambiguous. It is most often understood as an angered father sacrificing his son. I believe that one can understand this notion much better in terms of the experience of vulnerability accepted till the very end to the point of saying: "Here is my life given for you." With this second interpretation, there is no question of a more or less masochist self-denial. (Cf. Part I, chapters 3 and 5.)

SIN

In relation to the other, as to God, we experience the importance of the recognition of our limit, of our failure. The experience of sin is always linked to that of pardon, without which it becomes unhealthy remorse and isolation. As Pascal says, we only can meaningfully discover our sinfulness through the experience of being forgiven. (Cf. Part I, chapters 3 and 5; Part II, chapter 17.)

TO DO GOD'S WILL, NOT ONE'S OWN

While this aim has often been understood to mean that one has to deny oneself, this is not the meaning intended by Jesus in the Gospel. When Jesus refers to his Father's will, it seems to be in view of assuring his listeners that he does not impose his will on them. That is a condition of being a liberating person: not to impose one's will on others. That is why Jesus never spoke in his own name (even when he spoke with authority). He referred to the will of his Father who is presented as someone who wants all people to have life and joy abundantly. (Cf. Part I, chapter 3.)

1. Explain the metamorphoses of the spirit according to Nietzsche.

2. Relate these Nietzschean categories to the passage from justification by works to justification by faith.

3. What is the difference between the "camel's" image of God, and the "child's" image of God?